D1466357

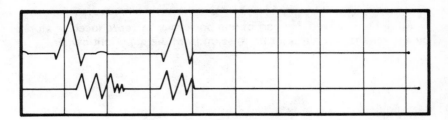

TERMINATING LIFE

Conflicting Values In Health Care

Gary E. McCuen
and
Therese Boucher

IDEAS IN CONFLICT SERIES

publications inc.

**411 Mallalieu Drive
Hudson, Wisconsin 54016**

Illustration & photo credits
M. G. Lord, Newsday 98, President's Commission for the Study of Ethical Problems in Medicine and Biomedical and Behavioral Research 20, 26, 39, 44, 54, 58, 66, 75, 103, 117, 122, 127, David Seavey, USA Today 11, 89, 112, 113, 137

©1985 by Gary E. McCuen Publications, Inc.
411 Mallalieu Drive • Hudson, Wisconsin 54016 •
(715) 386-5662
International Standard Book Number 0-86596-051-8
Printed in the United States of America

CONTENTS

CHAPTER 3   LIVING WILLS: Debating The Issue

CHAPTER 4   SAVING DEFECTIVE INFANTS: Ideas in Conflict

CHAPTER 5   ORGAN TRANSPLANTS AND HIGH-TECH MEDICINE: Pro and Con

REASONING SKILL DEVELOPMENT

These activities may be used as individualized study guides for students in libraries and resource centers or as discussion catalysts in small group and classroom discussions.

This series features ideas in conflict on political, social and moral issues. It presents counterpoints, debates, opinions, commentary and analysis for use in libraries and classrooms. Each title in the series uses one or more of the following basic elements:

Introductions that present an issue overview giving historic background and/or a description of the controversy.

Counterpoints and debates carefully chosen from publications, books, and position papers on the political right and left to help librarians and teachers respond to requests that treatment of public issues be fair and balanced.

Symposiums and forums that go beyond debates that can polarize and oversimplify. These present commentary from across the political spectrum that reflect how complex issues attract many shades of opinion.

A *global* emphasis with foreign perspectives and surveys on various moral questions and political issues that will help readers to place subject matter in a less culture-bound and ethno-centric frame of reference. In an ever shrinking and interdependent world, understanding and cooperation are essential. Many issues are global in nature and can· be effectively dealt with only by common efforts and international understanding.

Reasoning skill study guides and discussion activities provide ready made tools for helping with critical reading and evaluation of content. The guides and activities deal with one or more of the following:

RECOGNIZING AUTHOR'S POINT OF VIEW

INTERPRETING EDITORIAL CARTOONS

VALUES IN CONFLICT

WHAT IS EDITORIAL BIAS?

WHAT IS SEX BIAS?

WHAT IS POLITICAL BIAS?

WHAT IS ETHNOCENTRIC BIAS?

WHAT IS RACE BIAS?

WHAT IS RELIGIOUS BIAS?

From across *the political spectrum* varied sources are presented for research projects and classroom discussions. Diverse opinions in the series come from magazines, newspapers, syndicated columnists, books, political speeches, foreign nations, and position papers by corporations and non-profit institutions.

About the Editors

Gary E. McCuen is an editor and publisher of anthologies for public libraries and curriculum materials for schools. Over the past 14 years his publications of over 200 titles have specialized in social, moral and political conflict. They include books, pamphlets, cassettes, tabloids, filmstrips and simulation games, many of them designed from his curriculums during 11 years of teaching junior and senior high school social studies. At present he is the editor and publisher of the *Ideas in Conflict* series and the *Editorial Forum* series.

Therese Boucher is a professional educator and author of religious books and articles. Her background includes a BA degree in sociology from Anna Maria College, and a Master's Degree in religious education from Assumption College with a concentration in curricular development.

CHAPTER 1

TERMINATING LIFE: VALUES IN CONFLICT

READINGS

OVERVIEW

HUMAN VALUES AND HIGH-TECH MEDICINE

Ellen Goodman

Ellen Goodman is a political columnist for The Boston Globe. *In the following article, she describes two cases of people who had similar wishes in "right to die" cases. She describes how and why the court reached a different and opposite decision in each case. Her statement explains why the moral questions about terminating medical treatment are becoming so provocative and difficult to deal with.*

Points To Consider

1. What is the nature of the two different cases described by Ellen Goodman?
2. What did the court decide in each case?
3. Why did the court decide differently in each case?
4. Why is it difficult to apply a single moral yardstick in "right to die" cases?

*These stories raise questions that set our
minds to spinning. It would be easier if we
could apply a single moral yardstick.*

Boston 10-12

An 85-year-old man died in Syracuse, N.Y., last weekend. By
all accounts, G. Ross Henninger had lived a full life: college
president, author, technical counselor to the military, husband,
father.

Yet it could also be said that his life was cut short, that he
committed suicide in the Syracuse nursing home where he lived
since his stroke last May. He simply stopped eating 45 days before his death.

The private nursing-home administrators, caught between a
mandate to take care of their patients and a law that gives patients the right to refuse care, had taken his case to court. There,
Justice Miller of the State Supreme Court ruled that the nursing
home had neither the obligation nor the right to force-feed their
elderly patient.

The justice wrote, "This court is heavily burdened by these
questions . . . (but) I will not against his wishes, order this man
to be operated upon, and/or to be force-fed." A day later, the
man was dead of starvation.

But while the family of the elderly Henninger was planning his
funeral, on the other side of the country, in Riverside, Calif. a 26-
year-old woman, severely handicapped by cerebral palsy, was
still alive because she was being force-fed. Elizabeth Bouvia had
gone to a different judge in a different state. She sued for the
right to have medical help, painkillers and hygienic care, while
she starved to death. The judge denied her request in December,
and recently the doctors won the right to force-feed her as long
as she's in the hospital.

Here we have two people with the same wish—to die. Two
cases that consistently pit the right-to-life advocates against the
right-to-die advocates. Surely we can decide: either we should
or shouldn't intervene to prevent suicide. Either a person does
or doesn't have the right to end his or her own life.

Provocative Cases

But in fact, these cases are so provocative that I, like many
others, agree with both these opposite decisions. Having just
written disapproval of Bouvia's legal plea, I nevertheless ap-
prove of the ruling in Henninger's case.

10

By David Seavey, USA TODAY

We are so often told that our attitudes should remain consistent about issues, that we may easily forget the details of the human life at its center. It occurs to me now that our apparent inconsistencies may say the most about these questions of life and death. They remind us that we're dealing with individual lives.

Almost six decades separated Elizabeth Bouvia and G. Ross Henninger. Suicide, they say, is a permanent solution to a temporary problem. But the problems of an 85-year-old stroke victim are not temporary. His choice, like that of a terminal cancer patient, was to be respected.

Bouvia's physical condition isn't temporary either. But her depression may be. Any young woman who had just ended a marriage, lost the hope of child-bearing and belief in a career within the same year could be despairing. Wasn't there some ambiguity in her decision to seek suicidal help in a psychiatric ward?

There was a subtle legal difference as well between these two cases. The Bouvia case tested the right of a patient to prescribe her own medical treatment. The Henninger case tested the right of a patient to resist medical treatment. In both decisions, the courts chose the less intrusive path.

Right to Die

But when all is said and done, the courts were required to judge individually the seriousness of the illness, the permanence of the problem. They were asked to determine whether each person's desire to die was "rational."

It is disturbing, bewildering, to try to decipher someone's right to live or die on the basis of their age, their illness, their pain, their life expectancy, their psyche. Where do you draw the line between the 26-year-old and the 85-year-old, between rescuing one back into life and comforting another into death? At 50, 60, 70? For cancer, paralysis, stroke?

How long does it take before we believe that Bouvia has permanently, not temporarily, lost the will to live? One year, five years? How long can we force-feed a patient and how many measures can we take to prevent suicide?

These stories raise questions that set our minds to spinning. It would be easier if we could apply a single moral yardstick. But in the end, these cases must be judged as human tales, one by one, whether in a family setting or a hospital room or a courtroom.

At times there is simply no way to be both consistent and humane.

12

VALUES IN CONFLICT

A GENTLE AND EASY DEATH

South African Voluntary Euthanasia Society

*The South African Voluntary Euthanasia Society
(S.A.V.E.S.) was founded in 1974 by a nursing home
sister, Mrs. Sylvia Kean. There are presently over 8000
members of S.A.V.E.S. throughout the Republic of South
Africa. In the following statement, S.A.V.E.S. describes its
position on passive and active euthanasia, a medical bill
of rights and the living will.*

Points To Consider

1. What is meant by "a gentle and easy death?"
2. What distinction is made between passive and active euthanasia?
3. How is a living will used in South Africa?
4. How is the South African medical bill of rights described?

Excerpted from a pamphlet distributed by the South African Voluntary
Euthanasia Society, 1984.

The South African Voluntary Euthanasia Society (S. A. V. E. S.) wishes to ensure a gentle and easy death for those afflicted with an incurable or irrecoverable disease or injury and adequate relief from pain and discomfort by appropriate treatment.

We are a **passive** voluntary euthanasia society. Our objective is natural dying and not being kept alive **artificially** in the event of irreversible brain damage and end-stage terminal illness. We are not concerned with **active** euthanasia—that is illegal in South Africa anyway.

Objectives of Voluntary Passive Euthanasia

Euthanasia means "good death". Passive euthanasia means "natural dying/good death".

The South African Voluntary Euthanasia Society (S.A.V.E.S) wishes to ensure a gentle and easy death for those afflicted with an incurable or irrecoverable disease or injury and adequate relief from pain and discomfort by appropriate treatment. THIS IS HUMANISM.

S.A.V.E.S recommends that those individuals who are in agreement with its objectives should sign a "LIVING WILL" when they are in good health and of sound mind, stating unequivocally the expectation that the right to die with dignity will be respected, as set out in the LIVING WILL, namely:

"If the time comes when I can no longer take part in decisions for my own future, let this Declaration stand as the testament to my wishes:

If there is no reasonable prospect of my recovery from physical illness or impairment expected to cause me severe distress or to render me incapable of rational existence, I request that I be allowed to die and not be kept alive by artificial means and that I receive whatever quantity of drugs may be required to keep me free from pain or distress even if the moment of death is hastened."

IT MUST BE EMPHASIZED that the individual has the following rights:

1. The right to complete, understandable and clear information from the physician regarding the disease or injury from which he/she is suffering, and the proposed medical treatment. The individual has the right thereafter to consent to or to refuse treatment. This is what is meant by 'informed consent'. The doctor is obliged to obtain informed consent in order to treat

14

the patient, and the LIVING WILL is in fact valid informed consent.
2. The right to proper care.
3. The right to personal dignity and integrity.
4. The right not to suffer.

Bill of Rights

Each person has the right to decide whether or not to undergo treatment (for example, surgery, cobalt treatment, chemotherapy, renal (kidney) dialysis, etc.) or whether only pain-killing drugs are desired, or any other form of treatment, or no treatment at all.

Further, in the event of a patient suffering a severe cerebral hemorrhage (a severe stroke), or being involved in a motor accident involving irreversible brain damage, or in the case of severe brain damage with severe paralysis, the Living Will is of value in assisting the doctor on the course of action to be instituted (or discontinued) in the event of the patient no longer being able to exist rationally (that is, being a mindless human-being). Various tests are in use, of course, to establish irreversible brain damage, e.g. encephalograms, reflexes, eye examination, etc. (This is different from delirium which results from a high fever and is able to be treated).

Theological Ethics

X "Thou shalt not kill, but needst not strive officiously to keep alive" [Arthur Hugh Clough 1819–1861]. Passive voluntary euthanasia means that the patient has elected to die naturally and not to be kept alive artificially by tubes and machines once irreversible brain damage has rendered that person incapable of rational existence or once the patient has experienced impairment expected to cause severe distress.

Also, in the event of terminal illness that person has elected to receive whatever quantity of drugs may be required to keep him/her free from pain or distress, even if the moment of death is hastened. This involves pain control only, keeping within the legally permissable doses of medication.

Passive voluntary euthanasia is, therefore, natural dying and

---

Passive Euthanasia

Professor Christian Barnard, the South African heart transplant surgeon, says he has practiced "passive" euthanasia on terminal patients for years, including his own mother. He and his brother Marius, also a heart surgeon, have both agreed that under certain extreme medical conditions each would assist the other in taking his own life.

The admissions are made in a new book, "Good Life: Good Death" (Prentice Hall), to be published this week.

In it, Barnard is emphatic that he has never practiced active euthanasia, legally regarded as murder in many countries. But he argues that active euthanasia could have a definite place in the practice of medicine.

John Delin, *London Daily Telegraphy*, 1981

---

not mercy-killing (by means of overdosing, for example) which is illegal in South Africa and throughout the world (and which would be active euthanasia). It does not mean suicide either, which is unnatural dying.

Legality of the Living Will

It must be stressed that:

a) The Living Wills are entirely voluntary. Once the Living Will has been signed in the presence of two persons, both present together, it is a legal document. It can be cancelled if desired. Persons of 18 years of age and upwards can sign a Living Will.

b) Three originals of the Living Will are supplied initially, and should be dealt with as follows:

   i) One signed original of this document must be placed with one's personal papers at home, and its whereabouts made known to one's relatives/close friends;

   ii) The second original (also signed) should be kept for possible hospital/nursing home use and if admitted to a hospital/nursing home, should be handed to the Ward Sister concerned;

   iii) The third original (also signed) must be discussed with one's doctor, after which it should be placed by the doctor in one's medical file.

c) It is a good plan to look over the Living Will every year and make it clear to one's relatives/close friends and doctor that one's wishes are unchanged.

THE LEAST WORST DEATH

M. Pabst Battin

M. Pabst Battin, Ph.D. is associate professor of philosophy at the University of Utah. Work for this article, conducted at the Veterans Administration Medical Center, Salt Lake City, was sponsored by the Utah Endowment for the Humanities, Humanist-in-Residence Programs. She explains how the right-to-die movement may, in some cases, make death more painful.

Points To Consider

1. What is the one legally protected mechanism for achieving natural death?
2. Why is an earlier death not always an easier death?
3. When does "the right to die" go wrong?
4. What approach to "the right to die" question does the author advocate?

M. Pabst Battin, "The Least Worst Death," **The Hastings Center Report,** April, 1983, pp. 13-16.

The successes of the right-to-die movement have had a bitterly ironic result: institutional and legal protections for "natural death" have, in some cases, actually made it more painful to die.

In recent years "right-to-die" movements have brought into the public consciousness something most physicians have long known: that in some hopeless medical conditions, heroic efforts to extend life may no longer be humane, and the physician must be prepared to allow the patient to die. Physician responses to patients' requests for "natural death" or "death with dignity" have been, in general, sensitive and compassionate. But the successes of the right-to-die movement have had a bitterly ironic result: institutional and legal protections for "natural death" have, in some cases, actually made it more painful to die.

There is just one legally protected mechanism for achieving natural death: refusal of medical treatment. It is available to both competent and incompetent patients. In the United States, the competent patient is legally entitled to refuse medical treatment of any sort on any personal or religious grounds, except perhaps where the interests of minor children are involved. A number of court cases, including Quinlan, Saikewicz, Spring, and Eichner have established precedent in the treatment of an incompetent patient for a proxy refusal by a family member or guardian. In addition, eleven states now have specific legislation protecting the physician from legal action for failure to render treatment when a competent patient has executed a directive to be followed after he is no longer competent. A durable power of attorney, executed by the competent patient in favor of a trusted relative or friend, is also used to determine treatment choices after incompetence occurs.

An Earlier But Not Easier Death

In the face of irreversible, terminal illness, a patient may wish to die sooner but "naturally," without artificial prolongation of any kind. By doing so, the patient may believe he is choosing a death that is, as a contributor to the New England Journal of Medicine has put it, "comfortable, decent, and peaceful"; "natural death." . . . That is why he is willing to undergo death earlier and that is why, he assumes, natural death is legally protected. But the patient may conceive of "natural death" as more than pain-free; he may assume that it will allow time for reviewing life and saying farewell to family and loved ones, for last rites or final words, for passing on hopes, wisdom, confessions, and

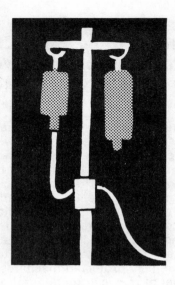

blessings to the next generation. These ideas are of course heavily stereotyped; they are the product of literary and cultural traditions associated with conventional death-bed scenes, reinforced by movies, books, and news stories, religious models, and just plain wishful thinking. Even the very term "natural" may have stereotyped connotations for the patient: something close to nature, uncontrived, and appropriate. As a result of these notions, the patient often takes "natural death" to be a painless, conscious, dignified, culminative slipping-away.

Now consider what sorts of death actually occur under the rubric of "natural death." . . .

Consider the bowel cancer patient with widespread metastases and a very poor prognosis who—perhaps partly out of consideration for the emotional and financial resources of his family—refuses surgery to reduce or bypass the tumor. How, exactly, will he die? This patient is clearly within his legal rights in refusing surgery, but the physician knows what the outcome is very likely to be: obstruction of the intestinal tract will occur, the bowel wall will perforate, the abdomen will become distended, there will be intractible vomiting (perhaps with a fecal character to the emesis), and the tumor will erode into adjacent areas, causing increased pain, hemorrhage, and sepsis. Narcotic sedation and companion drugs may be partially effective in controlling pain, nausea, and vomiting, but this patient will not get the kind of death he thought he had bargained for. Yet, he was willing to shorten his life, to use the single legally protected mechanism—refusal of treatment—to achieve that "natural" death.

20

Small wonder that many physicians are skeptical of the "gains" made by the popular movements supporting the right to die.

When the Right to Die Goes Wrong

Several distinct factors contribute to the backfiring of the right-to-die cause. First, and perhaps the most obvious, the patient may misjudge his own situation in refusing treatment or in executing a natural-death directive: his refusal may be precipitous and ill informed, based more on fear than on a settled desire to die . . .

But most important in the apparent backfiring of the right-to-die movement is the underlying ambiguity in the very concept of "natural death." Patients tend to think of the character of the experience they expect to undergo—a death that is "comfortable, decent, peaceful"—but all the law protects is the refusal of medical procedures. Even lawmakers sometimes confuse the two. The California and Kansas natural-death laws claim to protect what they romantically describe as "the natural process of dying." North Carolina's statute says it protects the right to a "peaceful and natural" death. But since these laws actually protect only refusal of treatment, they can hardly guarantee a peaceful, easy death. Thus, we see a widening gulf between the intent of the law to protect the patient's final desires, and the outcomes if the law is actually followed. The physician is caught in between: he recognizes his patient's right to die peacefully, naturally, and with whatever dignity is possible, but foresees the unfortunate results that may come about when the patient exercises this right as the law permits.

Of course, if the symptoms or pain become unbearable the patient may change his mind. The patient who earlier wished not to be "hooked up on tubes" now begins to experience difficulty in breathing or swallowing, and finds that a tracheotomy will relieve his distress. The bowel cancer patient experiences severe discomfort from obstruction, and gives permission for decompression or reductive surgery after all. In some cases, the family may engineer the change of heart because they find dying too hard to watch. Health care personnel may view these reversals with satisfaction: "See," they may say, "he really wants to live after all." But such reversals cannot always be interpreted as a triumph of the will to live; they may also be an indication that refusing treatment makes dying too hard.

Options for an Easier Death

How can the physician honor the dying patient's wish for a peaceful, conscious, and culminative death? There is more than one option . . .

The physician can do much to grant the dying patient the humane death he has chosen by using the sole legally protected mechanism that safeguards the right to die: refusal of treatment. This mechanism need not always backfire. For in almost any terminal condition, death can occur in various ways, and there are many possible outcomes of the patient's present condition. The patient who is dying of emphysema could die of respiratory failure, but could also die of cardiac arrest or untreated pulmonary infection. The patient who is suffering from bowel cancer could die of peritonitis following rupture of the bowel, but could also die of dehydration, of pulmonary infection . . .

The crucial point is that certain conditions will produce a death that is more comfortable, more decent, more predictable, and more permitting of conscious and peaceful experience than others. Some are better, if the patient has to die at all, and some are worse. Which mode of death claims the patient depends in part on circumstance and in part on the physician's response to conditions that occur. What the patient who rejects active euthanasia or assisted suicide may realistically hope for is this: the least worst death among those that could naturally occur. Not all unavoidable surrenders need involve rout; in the face of inevitable death, the physician becomes strategist, the deviser of plans for how to meet death most favorably.

He does so, of course, at the request of the patient, or, if the patient is not competent, the patient's guardian or kin. Patient autonomy is crucial in the notion of natural death. The physician could of course produce death by simply failing to offer a particular treatment to the patient. But to fail to offer treatment that might prolong life, at least when this does not compromise limited or very expensive resources to which other patients have claims, would violate the most fundamental principles of medical practice; some patients do not want "natural death," regardless of the physical suffering or dependency that prolongation of life may entail.

A scenario in which natural death is accomplished by the patient's selective refusal of treatment has one major advantage over active euthanasia and assisted suicide: refusal of treatment is clearly permitted and protected by law. Unfortunately, however, most patients do not have the specialized medical knowledge to use this self protective mechanism intelligently. Few are aware that some kinds of refusal of treatment will better serve their desires for a "natural death" than others. And few patients realize that refusal of treatment can be selective . . . Then, too, patients may be unable to distinguish therapeutic from palliative procedures. And they may not understand the interaction between one therapy and another. In short, most patients do not have enough medical knowledge to foresee the consequences of

> **The crucial point is that certain conditions will produce a death that is more comfortable, more decent, more predictable, and more permitting of conscious and peaceful experience than others.**

refusing treatment on a selective basis; it is this that the physician must supply . . .

The role of the physician as strategist of natural death may be even more crucial in longer-term degenerative illnesses, where both physician and patient have far more advance warning that the patient's condition will deteriorate, and far more opportunity to work together in determining the conditions of the ultimate death. Of course, the first interest of both physician and patient will be strategies for maximizing the good life left. Nevertheless, many patients with long-term, eventually terminal illnesses, like multiple sclerosis, Huntington's chorea, diabetes, or chronic renal failure, may educate themselves considerably about the expected courses of their illnesses, and may display a good deal of anxiety about the end stages. This is particularly true in hereditary conditions where the patient may have watched a parent or relative die of the disease. But it is precisely in these conditions that the physician's opportunity may be greatest for humane guidance in the unavoidable matter of dying. He can help the patient to understand what the long-term options are in refusing treatment while he is competent, or help him to execute a natural-death directive or durable power of attorney that spells out the particulars of treatment refusal after he becomes incompetent . . .

Flexibility

In both acute and long-term terminal illnesses, the key to good strategy is flexibility in considering all the possibilities at hand. These alternatives need not include active euthanasia or suicide measures of any kind, direct or indirect. To take advantage of the best of the naturally occurring alternatives is not to cause the patient's death, which will happen anyway, but to guide him away from the usual, frequently worst, end.

In the current enthusiasm for "natural death" it is not patient autonomy that dismays physicians. What does dismay them is the way in which respect for patient autonomy can lead to cruel results. The cure for that dismay lies in the realization that the physician can contribute to the genuine honoring of the patient's autonomy and rights, assuring him of "natural death" in the way in which the patient understands it, and still remain within the confines of good medical practice and the law.

23

4

VALUES IN CONFLICT

TERMINATING MEDICAL TREATMENT: POINTS AND COUNTERPOINTS

Sidney H. Wanzer et al. vs. Joan Beck

Physician guidelines for the responsibility of doctors toward hopelessly ill patients were described by Sidney Wanzer in The New England Journal of Medicine. *The guidelines were written by a distinguished group of physicians from leading national medical centers and educational institutions. Joan Beck is a nationally syndicated columnist and political commentator who felt these guidelines took a "chilling step" away from traditional values and ethics in health care for the dying.*

Points To Consider

1. What are the basic proposals in the physician guidelines for hopelessly ill patients?
2. How do the guidelines distinguish between competent patients and incompetent patients?
3. What specific criticisms of the physician guidelines does Joan Beck raise?
4. What does she say about living wills?

Sidney H. Wanzer, M.D., S. James Adelstein, M.D., Ronald E. Cranford, M.D., Daniel D. Federman, M.D., Edward D. Hook, M.D., Charles G. Moertel, M.D., Peter Safar, M.D., Alan Stone, M.D., Helen B. Taussig, M.D., and Jane van Eys, Ph.D., M.D., "The Physician's Responsibility Toward Hopelessly Ill Patients," **The New England Journal of Medicine,** April 2, 1984, pp. 955–59 and Joan Beck, "Pull-the-Plug Debate Takes Ugly Turn," **Chicago Tribune,** April 26, 1984. Reprinted by permission of **The New England Journal of Medicine** and the **Chicago Tribune.**

THE POINT—by Sidney Wanzer et al.

Efforts to define policies on withholding or withdrawing life-sustaining procedures from hopelessly ill patients are a relatively recent development. In 1976, when two major hospitals publicly announced their protocols in treating the hopelessly ill, the Journal marked the event with an editorial titled "Terminating Life Support: Out of the Closet!" ...

The patient's right to make decisions about his or her medical treatment is clear. That right, grounded in both common law and the constitutional right of privacy, includes the right to refuse life-sustaining treatment—a fact affirmed in the courts and recently supported by a presidential commission ...

Individualizing Treatment

The Competent Patient

In treating patients who are generally alert but are dying of a progressive illness, such as cancer, the physician must be especially sensitive to their need for relief from pain and suffering. Aggressive treatment in response to this need is often justified even if under other circumstances the risk of such treatment would be medically undesirable e.g., it would result in respiratory depression). The level of care to be provided should reflect an understanding between patient and physician and should be reassessed from time to time. In many cases neither intensive care nor emergency resuscitation is desired by the patient and his or her family; there may be a wish only for comfort, with general medical treatment given solely to provide relief from distress.

When the facilities provided by an acute-care hospital are not essential to the comfort and dignity of the dying patient, he or she should be moved to a more appropriate setting, if possible. Care at home or in a less regimented environment, such as a hospice, should be encouraged and facilitated.

The Incompetent Patient

Patients with brain death. Patients with irreversible cessation of all functions of the brain, determined in accordance with accepted medical standards, are considered medically and legally dead, and no further treatment is required.

Patients in a persistent vegetative state. In this state the neocortex is largely and irreversibly destroyed, although some brain-stem functions persist. When this neurologic condition has been established with a high degree of medical certainty and has been carefully documented, it is morally justifiable to with-

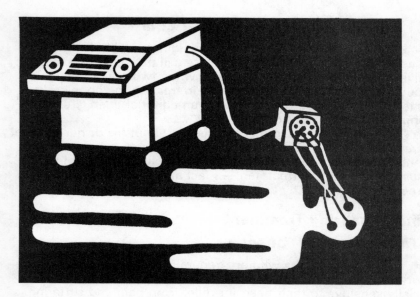

hold antibiotics and artificial nutrition and hydration, as well as other forms of life-sustaining treatment, allowing the patient to die. This obviously requires careful efforts to obtain knowledge of the patient's prior wishes and the understanding and agreement of the family. Family attitudes will clearly influence the type of care given in these cases.

Severely and irreversibly demented patients. Patients in this category, most of them elderly, are at one end of the spectrum of decreasing mental capacity. They do not initiate purposeful activity but passively accept nourishment and bodily care.

When the severely demented patient has previously made his or her wishes known and when there is intercurrent illness, it is ethically permissible for the physician to withhold treatment that would serve mainly to prolong the dying process. When there is no prior expression or living will and when no family or advocate is available, the physician should be guided by the need to provide the most humane kind of treatment and the need to carry out the patient's wishes insofar as they are ascertainable.

Severely and irreversibly demented patients need only care given to make them comfortable. If such a patient rejects food and water by mouth, it is ethically permissible to withhold nutrition and hydration artificially administered by vein or gastric tube. Spoon feeding should be continued if needed for comfort. It is ethically appropriate not to treat intercurrent illness except with measures required for comfort (e.g., antibiotics for pneumonia can be withheld). For this category of patients, it is best if decisions about the handling of intercurrent illness are made prospectively, before the onset of an acute illness or threat to life. The physician must always bear in mind that senseless perpetuation of the status quo is decision by default.

Elderly patients with permanent mild impairment of competence. Many elderly patients are described as "pleasantly senile." Although somewhat limited in their ability to initiate activities and communicate, they often appear to be enjoying their moderately restricted lives. Freedom from discomfort should be an overriding objective in the care of such a patient. If emergency resuscitation and intensive care are required, the physician should provide these measures sparingly, guided by the patient's prior wishes, if known, by the wishes of the patient's family, and by an assessment of the patient's prospects for improvement.

Conclusions

Few topics in medicine are more complicated, more controversial, and more emotionally charged than treatment of the hopelessly ill. Technology competes with compassion, legal precedent lags, and controversy is inevitable. The problem is least troublesome when an informed patient and an empathetic physician together confront a clearly defined outlook. We have tried to outline a reasonable approach that is useful even when these ideal circumstances do not obtain. Our recommendations cannot resolve all conflicts, provide simple formulas, or comprehensively address the wide range of issues involved in caring for the hopelessly ill patient, but they are intended to offer some clarification and support for those who bear the social responsibility of deciding whether to forgo life-sustaining treatment for the hopelessly ill.

THE COUNTERPOINT—by Joan Beck

Who should live, who should die and who should decide used to be a hush-hush issue limited to the terminally ill for whom respirators only can prolong dying and to hopelessly damaged newborns.

But last week, the New England Journal of Medicine pushed the debate into an ugly new area by publishing proposed guidelines for doctors that would limit medical care for the irreversibly ill and elderly in some deeply disturbing ways.

Distinguished Group

The physicians who drew up the guidelines are a distinguished group. They represent some of the nation's best-known medical schools and hospitals. The New England Journal of

Medicine is the country's most influential medical journal, noted for its thoughtful and comprehensive articles on the dilemmas posed by uncontrollable medical costs, new medical technologies and the growth of the medical-industrial complex. What these doctors propose will be taken seriously indeed.

Much of what the doctors prescribe is becoming familiar and accepted: Patients have the right to decide about their medical care, if competent to do so, even if it means ending treatment and accepting a death that could be postponed, the doctors comment. Patients are, however, owed information, comfort, dignity and release from distress if possible, the doctors say.

Ideally, people should make their wishes known in advance with a living will or by naming a surrogate to act for them if they were to become incompetent, the writers assert. A patient whose brain is dead is legally and medically dead and nothing more should be done, they say.

After that discussion, the physicians move into less comfortable areas: When a patient has slipped into a "persistent vegetative state," they suggest, it is morally justifiable to withhold antibiotics and intravenous nourishment and liquid, allowing the person to die. The doctors suggest that elderly people too senile to do much more than passively accept food and care need only to be made comfortable and that it is "ethically permissible" not to give them food and water by vein or gastric tube and to withhold treatment for other illnesses, such as pneumonia.

Most of us would make such decisions if a hopelessly ill loved one were dying. Most of us would make the same call for ourselves.

Chilling Step

But the physicians take one more chilling step for patients they call the "pleasantly senile." These, they say, are the elderly with "permanent mild impairment of competence" who "are somewhat limited in their ability to initiate activities and communicate" but who "often appear to be enjoying their moderately restricted lives."

"Freedom from discomfort should be an overriding objective in the care of such a patient," recommended the doctors. "If emergency resuscitation and intensive care are required, the physician should provide these measures sparingly, guided by the patient's prior wishes, if known, by the wishes of the patient's family and by an assessment of the patient's prospects for improvement."

The doctors spell out what they mean by care aimed only at making a patient comfortable. They say routine monitoring, such as daily temperature and blood pressure readings, need not be

28

done. Diagnostic tests can be stopped. So can antibiotics. Food and water given "naturally or artificially" may be provided or not, "depending on the patient's comfort."

Laced through the recommendations are repeated hopes that people will decide in advance whether they want to live or die if they are incurably ill or senile, make their wishes known and relieve doctors of such decisions. But physicians, they say, must act on a patient's behalf if necessary and should not let their own inner conflicts, unrealistic expectations, feelings of professional failure, fear of legal liability or "the rare report of a patient with a similar condition who survived" stand in the way.

The writers say doctors also should consider the possibility of financial ruin of the patient's family and the drain on medical resources for treating others.

The Slippery Slope

Deciding not to treat the irreversibly ill and elderly whose competence is only mildly impaired is a long moral, legal and medical distance from not resuscitating the terminally ill or from prolonging dying. It is an ugly, unconscionable step down that slippery slope to active euthanasia.

The words in the recommendations—such as "mild impairment of competence"—invite disastrous interpretation. So does the phrase "irreversibly ill," which could be stretched to include chronic disorders. Coupled with new studies that show Medicare spending increased seven times between 1970 and 1982, now costs taxpayers $55 billion a year and may go broke by 1990, the proposals could be viewed as a particularly nasty kind of cost-cutting.

Living wills used to be touted as a way people could protect themselves from pointless resuscitation when they are dying. Such documents soon may seem necessary too, to protect the aging and ill from being denied medical treatment should they show small signs of "mild impairment of competence." The elderly have enough worries without wondering whether their doctor is about to call them "pleasantly senile" and write them off.

THE HOSPICE HAVEN ALTERNATIVE

President's Commission

The President's Commission for the Study of Ethical Problems in Medicine and Biomedical and Behavioral Research produced a twelve volume work dealing with major issues in medical ethics. The following statement is taken from the volume titled Deciding to Forego Life-Sustaining Treatment *and deals with the advantages of hospice care for terminal patients.*

Points To Consider

1. What is the difference between a hospital, nursing home and hospice?
2. How do hospice programs vary?
3. Why have hospices in the U.S. and Great Britain tried to remain separate from traditional institutions like nursing homes and hospitals?
4. How has recent federal legislation helped the hospice movement financially in America?

Excerpted from **Deciding to Forego Life-Sustaining Treatment**, President's Commission for the Study of Ethical Problems in Medicine and Biomedical and Behavioral Research, March, 1983.

People entering hospice programs not only know they are sick but also that their death will occur quite soon.

Whereas patients entering hospitals usually do so expecting to be cured and people entering nursing homes expect to stay for considerable periods of time and may not even be sick, people entering hospice programs not only know they are sick but also that their death will occur quite soon. Before 1974 hospices were virtually unknown in the United States. Now this grassroots movement has spawned an estimated 800 programs across the country. Hospices were developed for the sole purpose of assisting dying patients—typically cancer patients who have exhausted all reasonable forms of curative treatment—to live their remaining weeks or months as free of symptoms and as much in control as possible. They have been deliberately created as an alternative to traditional long-term care institutions.

Hospices are further distinguished from hospitals and nursing homes by several features. First, the term "hospice" refers not to a building, but to a concept of care. Thus a hospice is a social and health care "institution," but not necessarily an inpatient facility. In the United States, most hospice care is delivered to people in their homes and many hospice programs provide only home care. Second, the patient and his or her family are considered to be the unit of care. Third, attention is given not only to physical needs, but also to emotional, social, and spiritual needs. Finally, hospice care is delivered by multidisciplinary teams of providers, including volunteers, on whom the hospice movement has depended heavily.

Programs Vary

Hospice programs vary substantially in their administrative arrangements and service offerings. However, all hospices share a philosophy of care. Hospice development has been premised on the belief that home is almost always the best place to die and that traditional medical care facilities, especially acute care hospitals, are inappropriate to the needs of the dying as well as unnecessarily costly. They support families not only in their care of the patient but emotionally throughout a period of bereavement.

Like all other institutions, hospices have their particular ethos and operate under some constraints that necessarily impinge on the range of options available to patients and the ease of obtaining them. To their credit, hospices have been more self-conscious and self-critical than traditional institutions about these effects on patients. Because they recognize that their orientation differs from the norm in health care today, most hospices discuss their philosophy and approach with potential patients and their families in order to enhance patient self-determination; many have rather explicit formal consent procedures. Nonetheless, some patients do not realize that hospice admission amounts to a decision to forego many kinds of life-sustaining treatment (such as resuscitation, continuous cardiovascular monitoring, or chemotherapy).

Hospices in this country, as in Great Britian, have deliberately tried to remain separate from traditional institutions. When physically or administratively linked to them, hospices have taken steps to minimize the influence of the parent institutions. Hospice programs do have certain difficulties of their own. First, their institutional separateness can erect a hurdle to patients' reentering the traditional care setting should such a step become necessary or desirable. Second, although hospices pride themselves on providing an alternative to the norms embodied in acute care hospitals, their own norms and philosophy of care may make it emotionally (even if not practically) difficult to offer their patients some alternatives. For example, the enthusiasm and personal involvement of care givers—at hospices as at other institutions—can make patients feel guilty if they reject recommendations, resist plans of care, fail to respond to treatment (that is, report symptom relief), or fail to conform to institutional norms (which is a general acceptance of death). In contrast to hospitals that sometimes pressure patients to continue aggressive therapy after it has ceased to be warranted, hospices risk pressuring patients to accept death too readily and to forego potentially life-sustaining therapies too quickly.

Federal Legislation

Until recently hospices have not had a firm financial base, relying instead on volunteers (both lay and professional), charitable donations, occasional demonstration grants from Federal agencies, and (rarely) reimbursement by third-party payors on an experimental basis. Federal legislation passed in September 1982 will enable hospice services to be reimbursed under Medicare. With this precedent, other third-party payors are expected to follow suit. Unfortunately, the legislation's requirements and incentives are likely to promote substantial and unjustified inequities in access to hospice care. For example, the requirement that, in order to qualify for this coverage, patients must be expected to die within six months, favors hospice care (which is of higher quality than that available to other elderly patients under Medicare). Also, this reimbursement policy will favor cancer patients, since they include the largest group of patients for whom prognostication of death within a few months can be made with acceptable reliability.

Several other concerns have been raised as a result of the recent legislation. If hospice programs become readily available, especially as a desirable place to send "failed" patients, hospital physicians and social workers may alter the care of patients in order to qualify them for hospice admission. Commentators also fear that hospices will become big business, as the nursing home industry did when its financial base became secure, and lose their special value for dying patients. In addition, if hospices are more generally available, efforts in traditional institutions to improve care of the dying might be slowed or abandoned altogether. "Experts in dying" may be created just as experts in caring for the elderly have been, and care could be further fragmented. Moreover, if hospice care is found to be less expensive than traditional care for at least some discernable categories of patients, pressure may build for certain groups of patients to be limited to hospices or to have reimbursement provided at a rate no greater than for hospice care, thereby effectively denying those patients the alternative of more aggressive treatment.

The present virtues of hospices may depend upon the special commitment of dedicated care givers who have pioneered in this field. Mechanisms for careful and sensitive review should be part of present planning efforts if the benefits now offered by hospices are to be maintained when these facilities become a larger feature of patient care. The needed review will be unusual in that it must aim to monitor quality of care in such important but unfamiliar terms as whether the patient's role in decision-making is being fostered and whether death is, as far as possible, appropriate to the particular person's situation.

VALUES IN CONFLICT

*This activity may be used as an individualized study
guide for students in libraries and resource centers
or as a discussion catalyst in small group and classroom
discussions.*

Guidelines

Read each case carefully. Then decide what you would do if
you were responsible for the patient's treatment in each
situation. Discuss the reasons for your answers after you have
considered the questions below.

1. Which case presents the most difficult problems?

2. Do you think legal problems might arise from a particular
   decision in any case?

3. Which case would be the least difficult to deal with?

CASE ONE: A twelve year old girl suffers from deadly bone
cancer. Her preacher father forbids chemotherapy and
radiation on the football-sized leg tumor, for religious
reasons. Without it she will die in three months. The
girl has mixed feelings about the decision. What would
you decide if you were the appellate judge?

CASE TWO: A pregnant woman suffers a fatal seizure and is
declared clinically dead, after several hours on life
support systems. At the time of the seizure she is 22
weeks pregnant. If she is fed intravenously and given
antibiotics for 60 days, there is some chance that a
Caesarean section would yield a healthy baby. If you
were the husband or mother of the brain-dead woman
would you authorize life support or turn off the
machinery?

CASE THREE: Mac is a middle aged cop who finds out he has
lung cancer. After 6 months he is wasted away to 60 lbs
and kept alive by IV's and oxygen piped into a mask. In
one month's time, he is resuscitated 52 times after his
breathing stops. The hospital rules are that the nurse
call in a team to resuscitate him as many times as
necessary. Mac himself is begging the nurse and his
wife not to allow any more attempts to save him. The
pain is out of control. One more code blue happens. If
you were the nurse would you call in the team to
resuscitate or not?

*I must tell what
I would do —
NO*

35

CHAPTER 2

ASSISTED SUICIDE, EUTHANASIA AND MERCY KILLING: POINTS AND COUNTERPOINTS

READINGS

6

THE POINT

EUTHANASIA IS A FUNDAMENTAL RIGHT

Voluntary Euthanasia Society of London

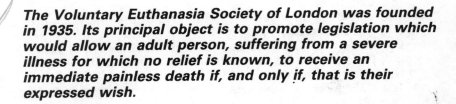

The Voluntary Euthanasia Society of London was founded in 1935. Its principal object is to promote legislation which would allow an adult person, suffering from a severe illness for which no relief is known, to receive an immediate painless death if, and only if, that is their expressed wish.

Points to Consider

1. How is euthanasia defined?
2. What are the misunderstandings about euthanasia?
3. What specifically does The Voluntary Euthanasia Society (VES) advocate?
4. How is the Suicide Act of 1961 defined?
5. What kind of legislation is needed?

Excerpted from **The Last Right,** a pamphlet by The Voluntary Euthanasia Society of London, 1984.

When the alternatives are death with dignity, or death accompanied by prolonged pain and distress, common sense as well as compassion support our demand that the choice should belong to the individual.

Euthanasia is defined in the Oxford Dictionary as "gentle and easy death: bringing about of this, especially in case of incurable and painful disease". The Voluntary Euthanasia Society believes that this should be the lawful right of the individual, in carefully defined circumstances and with the utmost safeguards, if, **and only if,** that is his expressed wish.

Misunderstandings and Misrepresentations

One would expect general approval of such a humane and compassionate aim. There is, indeed, ample evidence of rapidly growing support in this country and overseas. But as the campaign to legalize voluntary euthanasia gathers support and momentum so does the campaign of our opponents.

The purpose of this booklet is to state the case for voluntary euthanasia. Before attempting this, however, it is desirable to dispose of three of the most common misunderstandings and misrepresentations.

- The VES does not advocate getting rid of the old, the infirm and the unwanted'.
  On the contrary, the Society believes that the care of the old, the sick and the dying should be a paramount obligation upon any humane society.
- The VES does not advocate the 'putting down' of handicapped babies, or the mentally retarded. We seek only the legalization of voluntary euthanasia.
- The VES does not advocate 'suicide on demand', nor is it prepared to act in breach of the existing law. Under no circumstances, therefore, can the Society help anyone to commit suicide, either by giving direct assistance, or by providing personal advice or information about suicide methods.

Is Voluntary Euthanasia Necessary?

Despite great advances in medical knowledge, dying—which should be the natural and dignified end of life—is far too often a painful, prolonged and distressing process. Most people know of someone dear to them whose life has ended in this way and for whom death was a happy release. There is, indeed, ample justification for concern about the process of dying. It is not the fact

38

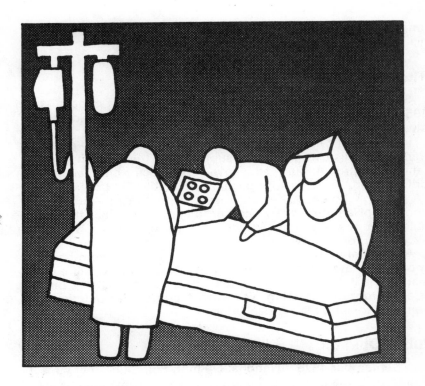

of dying that worries people; it is fear of the manner of dying, or of being kept 'alive' in such a pitiful condition that death would be infinitely preferable.

Victims of cancer often have to suffer severe and continuous distress. Pain can be reduced by the repeated use of narcotics and sedative drugs, but often at the cost of nausea, constipation, deterioration of the personality, and other distressing side effects. In addition to pain, victims of cancer may have to suffer the mental misery associated with the presence of a foul fungating growth, obstruction of the bowels, or incontinence, and the utter frustration that makes each day and night a death in life.

Diseases of the nervous system all too often lead to crippling paralysis or inability to walk, to severe headaches, to blindness and to the misery of incontinence and bedsores. Bronchitis, with its interminable cough and progressive shortness of breath, can have its special terrors which medical treatment can do little to abate in the later stages. Likewise, a patient with a stroke may be conscious but helpless. His misery is frequently overlooked.

When the alternatives are death with dignity, or death accompanied by prolonged pain and distress, common sense as well as compassion support our demand that the choice should be-

39

long to the individual. As the law now stands he has no choice; his wishes count for nothing . . .

The 1961 Suicide Act

Since the enactment of the Suicide Act (without opposition) in 1961, it is no longer a criminal offence to commit suicide or to attempt to do so.

Insofar as it recognized the right of the individual to determine when his own life was insupportable, this was an important development. But it still leaves both doctor and patient in a difficult and unsatisfactory position, since the Act provides that "A person who aids, abets, counsels or procures the suicide of another, or an attempt by another to commit suicide, shall be liable on conviction on indictment to imprisonment for a term not exceeding fourteen years."

A terminal patient suffering extreme distress seldom has the knowledge, the means or the capacity to end his own life, particularly if he is in hospital. He needs the aid of a doctor to obtain release from his suffering. Yet if the doctor carries out his patient's wishes he risks prosecution.

Public Opinion

In September 1976 a National Opinion Poll found that 69% agreed that 'the law should allow adults to receive medical help to an immediate peaceful death if suffering from incurable illness that is intolerable to them, provided they have previously requested such help in writing'. Only 17% disagreed.

Every Christian denomination produced a majority in favor. 72% of Anglicans, 71% of Methodists, 77% of members of the Church of Scotland, and 54% of Roman Catholics were in agreement. It was clearly shown that among Christians, as among the population as a whole, only a small minority oppose the legalisation of voluntary euthanasia.

A second question asked the same people whether they had known someone who had suffered within the previous five years from such an illness. 37% said that they had, thus emphasizing the current reality of the problem.

In November 1978, another National Opinion Poll asked the following question: 'Do you agree that, if a patient is suffering from a distressing and incurable physical illness, a doctor should be allowed to supply that patient with the means to end his own life, if the patient wishes to?' Since this question was more specifically concerned with suicide, there was slightly less support. Even so, 62% of the general public agreed, and only 22% disagreed—a majority of three to one. There was also majority support among all religious denominations except Roman Catholics, who were evenly divided.

The 1969 Bill and the Draft 1983 Bill

In 1969 the House of Lords debated the Voluntary Euthanasia Bill, based largely on a draft prepared by the Society. Its main provision was a form of written declaration requesting the administration of euthanasia, in carefully defined circumstances, in the event of the declarant suffering from an incurable and distressing disease or disability. This advance declaration was intended to meet the needs of terminal patients and of others suffering great distress from incurable illness.

The Bill proposed to authorize doctors to give euthanasia to a patient who, at least 30 days previously, had made such a written declaration before two witnesses. Two doctors, one of them a consultant, would have to certify that the patient was suffering from a painful and incurable physical disease. The declaration would preferably be made when the patient was in good health, long before the onset of the disease, and could be cancelled at any time. The 30 day waiting period would provide a built-in safeguard against impulsive or reluctant decisions.

The Bill received substantial support—40 votes for, 61 against. Among the opposition there were expressions of sympathy with the principle, but reservations on particular points.

A new draft Bill, broadly on the same lines as the 1969 Bill, was prepared during 1983. We hope it may be possible to introduce this in the House of Lords during the 1984/85 Parliamentary session.

The Need for Legislation

It has been said that there is no need for legalized voluntary euthanasia because, with the discovery of so many new drugs and techniques, a patient's pain and distress can be almost completely alleviated. The only need some say, is for more specialist hospices for the dying.

Even in hospices, some patients obtain inadequate relief from pain and distress. Breathlessness, vomiting, difficulty in swallowing, bedsores, surface tumors, wasting, incontinence and other miseries can all be ameliorated by devoted nursing, but this will not satisfy the patient who wants a clean death. A patient who continually needs another person to wipe his nose, stop his tongue from hanging out or change his sheets, may find it more dignified to opt for death.

There would still, therefore, be a need for voluntary euthanasia even if every terminal patient could be cared for in a hospice. Not everyone wants to spend his last weeks, months or years in an institution, however benevolent. Many want to die at home.

41

EUTHANASIA VIOLATES HUMAN LIFE

The Vatican

The following statement called the "Declaration on Euthanasia, the Sacred Congregation for the Doctrine of Faith" presents the official position of the Catholic Church on euthanasia. It explains the moral reasons for the Catholic Church's opposition to the concept of euthanasia.

Points to Consider

1. What are crimes against life as defined by the Second Vatican Ecumenical Council?
2. How is human life defined?
3. What is the definition of euthanasia?
4. Why is euthanasia opposed under all circumstances?

Excerpted from the "Declaration on Euthanasia, the Sacred Congregation for the Doctrine of the Faith," Vatican City (May 5, 1980).

Intentionally causing one's own death, or suicide, is equally as wrong as murder; such an action on the part of a person is to be considered as a rejection of God's sovereignty and loving plan.

The rights and values pertaining to the human person occupy an important place among the questions discussed today. In this regard, the Second Vatican Ecumenical Council solemnly reaffirmed the lofty dignity of the human person, and in a special way his or her right to life. The Council therefore condemned crimes against life "such as any type of murder, genocide, abortion, euthanasia, or wilful suicide."

More recently, the Sacred Congregation for the Doctrine of the Faith has reminded all the faithful of Catholic teaching on procured abortion. The Congregation now considers it opportune to set forth the Church's teaching on euthanasia.

The Value of Human Life

Human life is the basis of all goods, and is the necessary source and condition of every human activity and of all society. Most people regard life as something sacred and hold that no one may dispose of it at will, but believers see in life something greater, namely a gift of God's love, which they are called upon to preserve and make fruitful. And it is this latter consideration that gives rise to the following consequences:

1. No one can make an attempt on the life of an innocent person without opposing God's love for that person, without violating a fundamental right, and therefore without commiting a crime of the utmost gravity.

2. Everyone has the duty to lead his or her life in accordance with God's plan. That life is entrusted to the individual as a good that must bear fruit already here on earth, but that finds its full perfection only in eternal life.

3. Intentionally causing one's own death, or suicide, is therefore equally as wrong as murder; such an action on the part of a person is to be considered as a rejection of God's sovereignty and loving plan. Furthermore, suicide is also often a refusal of love for self, the denial of the natural instinct to live, a flight from the duties of justice and charity owed to one's neighbour, to various communities or to the whole of society—although, as is generally recognized, at times there are psychological factors present that can diminish responsibility or even completely remove it.

However, one must clearly distinguish suicide from that sacrifice of one's life whereby for a higher cause, such as God's glory, the salvation of souls or the service of one's brethren, a person offers his or her own life or puts it in danger.

Euthanasia

In order that the question of euthanasia can be properly dealt with, it is first necessary to define the words used.

In ancient times euthanasia meant an easy death without severe suffering. Today one no longer thinks of this original meaning of the word, but rather of some intervention of medicine whereby the sufferings of sickness or of the final agony are reduced, sometimes also with the danger of suppressing life prematurely. Ultimately, the word euthanasia is used in a more particular sense to mean "mercy killing", for the purpose of putting an end to extreme suffering, or saving abnormal babies, the mentally ill or the incurably sick from the prolongation, perhaps

44

for many years, of a miserable life, which could impose too heavy a burden on their families or on society.

It is therefore necessary to state clearly in what sense the word is used in the present document.

By euthanasia is understood an action or an omission which of itself or by intention causes death, in order that all suffering may in this way be eliminated. Euthanasia's terms of reference, therefore, are to be found in the intention of the will and in the methods used.

It is necessary to state firmly once more that nothing and no one can in any way permit the killing of an innocent human being, whether a fetus or an embryo, an infant or an adult, an old person, or one suffering from an incurable disease, or a person who is dying. Furthermore, no one is permitted to ask for this act of killing, either for himself or herself or for another person entrusted to his or her care, nor can he or she consent to it, either explicitly or implicitly. Nor can any authority legitimately recommend or permit such an action. For it is a question of the violation of the divine law, an offense against the dignity of the human person, a crime against life, and an attack on humanity.

It may happen that, by reason of prolonged and barely tolerable pain, for deeply personal or other reasons, people may be led to believe that they can legitimately ask for death or obtain it for others. Although in these cases the guilt of the individual may be reduced or completely absent, nevertheless the error of judgment into which the conscience falls, perhaps in good faith, does not change the nature of this act of killing, which will always be in itself something to be rejected. The pleas of gravely ill people who sometimes ask for death are not to be understood as implying a true desire for euthanasia; in fact it is almost always a case of an anguished plea for help and love. What a sick person needs, besides medical care, is love, the human and supernatural warmth with which the sick person can and ought to be surrounded by all those close to him or her, parents and children, doctors and nurses . . .

Withdrawing Treatment

It is also permissible to make do with the normal means that medicine can offer. Therefore one cannot impose on anyone the obligation to have the recourse to a technique which is already in use but which carries a risk or is burdensome. Such a refusal is not the equivalent of suicide; on the contrary, it should be considered as an acceptance of the human condition, or a wish to avoid the application of a medical procedure disproportionate to the results that can be expected, or a desire not to impose excessive expense on the family or the community.

The Euthanasia War

It is quite possible for the euthanasia "war" to be won or lost without any spectacular "battles". The public could easily be soothed by reassuring rhetoric or the feeling that the debate involves only "death with dignity". Under the resulting rhetorical fog, physicians could simply start practicing "mercy killing". Such a de facto euthanasia policy (like the de facto abortion policies which existed in many sectors of the medical community before the Supreme Court decision), together with some quiet pro-euthanasia court decisions, could mean an early victory for the pro-euthanasia forces.

Minnesota Citizens Concerned for Life, 1983

When inevitable death is imminent in spite of the means used, it is permitted in conscience to take the decision to refuse forms of treatment that would only secure a precarious and burdensome prolongation of life, so long as the normal care due to the sick person in similar cases is not interrupted. In such circumstances the doctor has no reason to reproach himself with failing to help the person in danger.

The norms contained in the present Declaration are inspired by a profound desire to serve people in accordance with the plan of the Creator. Life is a gift of God, and on the other hand death is unavoidable; it is necessary therefore that we, without in any way hastening the hour of death, should be able to accept it with full responsibility and dignity. It is true that death marks the end of our earthly existence, but at the same time it opens the door to immortal life. Therefore all must prepare themselves for this event in the light of human values, and Christians even more so in the light of faith.

As for those who work in the medical profession, they ought to neglect no means of making all their skill available to the sick and the dying; but they should also remember how much more necessary it is to provide them with the comfort of boundless kindness and heartfelt charity.

THE POINT

ASSISTED SUICIDE SHOULD BE LEGAL

Voluntary Euthanasia Society of New South Wales

The Voluntary Euthanasia Society of Victoria, Australia (VESV) is part of the world euthanasia movement. It is active in Australia promoting legislation to legalize voluntary euthanasia, assisted suicide and the right to refuse medical treatment. The following statement presents the society's position on assisted suicide and voluntary euthanasia.

Points to Consider

1. How is assisted suicide defined?
2. Why does the society advocate the legalization of assisted suicide?
3. How many different types of euthanasia are described?
4. What is the meaning of the term "mercy killing?"

Excerpted from **Voluntary Euthanasia: The Right to Choose,** a pamphlet by the Voluntary Euthanasia Society of New South Wales, 1982.

He recognized that the simplest way to decriminalize assisted suicide was to exempt from prosecution the abettor who had a compassionate and selfless motive.

It has seemed obvious to many campaigners over the years that if the incurably suffering person has the right to have another willing person end his life (euthanasia), that right must include the freedom to end his own life (suicide). Moreover, many such people would prefer to end their lives with medical help rather than place this responsibility on others. Indeed it may be argued that only if incapacity prevents suicide is euthanasia necessary.

For this reason V.E.S.V. has always included assisted suicide as an option in its proposals for law reform. It prefers to include it within the restrictions imposed by a v.e. Act (i.e. available only to the incurably suffering) because of the tragic resort to suicide in recent years especially by young people for often irrational and emotional reasons. V.E.S.V. therefore holds to the right of rational suicide, but abhors the needless loss of life by young people who are not given the help they need to enhance their capacity to value and enjoy living.

To use this tragedy as a reason for not reforming the suicide law is, however, a double tragedy. Preventing the rational and incurably suffering from choosing good dying is to force them to inexpert, unpleasant and botched attempts at suicide. If the emphasis was placed on self-determination for the rational and incurably ill, and on professional help for those capable of a desirable existence after overcoming emotional and social difficulties, good dying and good living would result.

The Law

Except in New South Wales suicide has been decriminalized in all Australian states. Attempted suicide is still an offence, although rarely prosecuted in N.S.W., South Australia, Queensland and Western Australia. Only in Tasmania and Victoria are attempted suicide (except in a suicide pact) and suicide both decriminalized. New Zealand has decriminalized both suicide and attempted suicide.

The decriminalization of suicide and attempted suicide has not softened the law's attitude to assisting suicide, which is punishable by a maximum term of life imprisonment in N.S.W., Queensland and Western Australia; in Tasmania the prison term is at the discretion of the magistrate.

In New Zealand and Victoria the law is similar to the British 1961 Suicide Act. A maximum 14 years imprisonment is provided for anyone who (in the words of Victoria's 1967 amendment to the Crimes Act) "aids, abets, counsels or incites" a suicide. The British Act uses the term "procure" rather than "incite".

In certain overseas non-British nations—Belgium, France, Germany, the Netherlands and Italy—compassionate motive has been recognized as an extenuation in cases of both euthanasia and assisted suicide. In Uraguay and Peru a person who aids and abets a suicide from altruistic motive is exempt from penalty. Swiss law provides token punishment in such cases.

The failure of legislatures to reform the law to permit v.e. or assisted suicide for the incurably suffering, despite the indisputable public approval of reform, has disillusioned many campaigners abroad, and encouraged a search for remedies outside statutory channels. It has also encouraged the idea that the demand for good dying should not involve the medical profession directly, and that people who want good dying should look to it themselves.

Scotland was the first country to produce a "guide." Scottish Exit was formed in 1980. Scottish Exit published **How to Die With Dignity** in August 1980.

Definitions and Explanatory Notes

Euthanasia:

1. A gentle, distress-free death (from the Greek "eu-thanatos", meaning literally "good death").
2. The inducement of this, especially in the case of incurable and painful illness or disability.

Euthanasia in its literal sense—a gentle death—is what all people hope for as a natural end to life. Euthanasia in the sense of inducing death is illegal. To bring what should be a natural blessing to those who would not otherwise have it requires the legalization of voluntary euthanasia.

Voluntary Euthanasia:

Voluntary euthanasia is the ending of a person's life at his earnest request when he suffers from incurably distressing illness or disability.

Note: The v.e. societies seek the legalization only of voluntary euthanasia in the case of incurable, distressing illness or disability or the actual or impending permanent loss of mental capacity.

Mercy Killing

"Mercy killing" is taking the life of another person who is suffering greatly without their permission. Whereas the problem we are addressing here, ethically and legally, is assistance in suicide upon request from a person who has good reason to need it.

Derek Humphrey, "Assisted Suicide: The Compassionate Crime", *Los Angeles Times,* July, 1982

Non-Voluntary Euthanasia:

Euthanasia administered to a person without his consent.
Note: This is not proposed by any v.e. societies. Their policy exclusively seeks the alleviation of distress in those who can choose death for themselves, and whose choice is presently denied them by law.

Compulsory Euthanasia:

Non-voluntary euthanasia imposed by authority.
Note: Opponents claim that voluntary euthanasia must degenerate into compulsory euthanasia. They point to Nazi atrocities which were called "euthanasia" at the time. No evidence can support this objection, however. Nazi atrocities were not legal; not voluntary; not good dying and therefore not euthanasia; not concerned to alleviate suffering or to support the citizen's right of self-determination; and the innocent were not protected by the type of legal safeguards proposed by the v.e. societies. Indeed, Nazism has one thing in common with opposition to voluntary euthanasia: both deny the citizen's free choice about his own life and death.

"Passive" Euthanasia:

The inducement of gentle death by the non-use or withdrawal of treatment necessary to sustain life.
Note: "Passive" is a misnomer, since the decision to withdraw treatment is a deliberate act. It is "passive" only in the sense that death is primarily due to "natural causes". This is widely practised now and without legal regulation. Death is induced by, for example, (a) the switching off of respirators in intensive care units when recovery is deemed impossible, (b) the non-use of antibiotics to cure infection where a patient is in the

50

final stage of fatal illness, and (c) the nonventilation or starvation of deformed babies (not always a "gentle" death). Because in all these cases the patient dies of "natural causes" the doctor may escape prosecution, unless neglect is alleged.

"Active" Euthanasia:

The inducement of gentle death solely by means without which life would continue naturally.

Note: Death may be induced by, for example, a massive dose of morphine. Since death cannot be attributed to "natural causes" "active" euthanasia is not easily concealed from the law. The most obviously illegal form of euthanasia, it is the quickest and most painless, and is therefore the one whose legalization is most needed.

"Indirect" Euthanasia:

A gentle death caused by treatment for pain or other symptoms which has as a side effect the shortening of life.

Note: This form of "active" euthanasia, because it does not primarily intend death, which is the legal criterion of guilt in homicide, is the only form of euthanasia that can claim to be legal. It is also the only form of "active" euthanasia advocated by medical authorities.

"Mercy-killing".

The term "euthanasia" is preferred to the more common "mercy-killing" because (a) "mercy-killing" does not necessarily include the idea of gentle death, (b) "mercy-killing" is (erroneously) thought by many people to mean non-voluntary euthanasia, and (c) "mercy" is a paternalistic expression inappropriate to the case: voluntary euthanasia is a citizen's right, not the exercise of someone's "mercy". The American philosopher Marvin Kohl has partly overcome this last objection by coining the term "kindly killing".

Suicide:

To end one's own life.

Note: Voluntary euthanasia is sometimes inaccurately called a form of suicide. It is true that in both cases death is desired by the person whose life is at issue, but the difference lies in the identity of the killer. Any voluntary euthanasia legislation should allow an incurably suffering patient who prefers to administer the means of his own death to obtain assistance from his doctor for that purpose.

SOCIETY MUST PROHIBIT INTENTIONAL KILLING

President's Commission

The President's Commission for the Study of Ethical Problems in Medicine and Biomedical and Behavioral Research produced a twelve volume work dealing with major issues in medical ethics. The following statement is taken from the volume titled Deciding to Forego Life-Sustaining Treatment *and deals with the legal prohibitions of assisted suicides by physicians.*

Points to Consider

1. What is said about decisions to forego life-sustaining treatment?
2. What does the law say about a physician who intentionally takes the life of a patient who wants to die?
3. Under what circumstances is killing free from legal sanctions?
4. What is the legal status of suicide?

Excerpted from **Deciding to Forego Life-Sustaining Treatment,** President's Commission for the Study of Ethical Problems in Medicine and Biomedical and Behavioral Research, March, 1983.

A physician's shooting or poisoning of a dying patient, even at the patient's request and from merciful motives, falls within the definition of murder.

Regardless of how interests are weighed in specific cases, a decision to forego life-sustaining treatment has been firmly established as a Constitutionally protected right that can be overcome only by marshalling countervailing considerations of substantial weight. In practice, these countervailing considerations are reflected in and implemented by the sanctions and procedures of criminal, civil, and administrative law.

Criminal Law.

Throughout the ages almost all cultures have regarded the protection of human life as a major aim of their legal systems. In the Anglo-American tradition, proscriptions of homicide and suicide are fundamental components of the criminal law. Yet no such legal proscription is absolute. Self-defense, the defense of others, killing in the conduct of military activities, and capital punishment are among the well-established justifications and excuses for homicide. Criminal law applies these same general norms to physicians and other health care professionals, not only in their capacity as ordinary citizens, but also in their professional capacities.

The criminal law confines people's freedom of action, in order to protect society, in ways that civil law does not. Although a patient's "informed consent" is sufficient authority in the civil law for a medical intervention, consent is never accepted as a defense to the crime of murder. An individual who seeks death at the hands of another, regardless of the reason, does not confer immunity from prosecution on the one who takes the life, because the taking of innocent human life is seen as a wrong to the entire society, not just to the dead person. A physician's shooting or poisoning of a dying patient, even at the patient's request and from merciful motives, falls within the definition of murder.

In some situations the criminal law looks to other branches of the law to fill in the details of punishable conduct. The law ordinarily holds individuals liable only for the injurious consequences of their acts, not for the injurious consequences of omissions of action. If someone throws into deep water a person who is known to be unable to swim and the nonswimmer then drowns, criminal and civil liability will be imposed. But if someone merely happens to be present when another is having

53

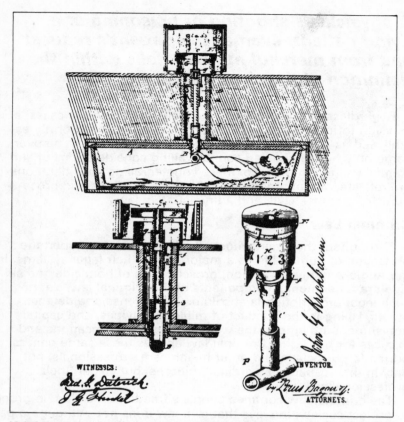

Krichbaum's device for indicating life in buried persons, Patent Sketch, 1882.

obvious difficulty swimming in deep water, and if he or she is the only other person present and could rescue the drowning individual, that person ordinarily has no legal obligation to do so—although the failure to rescue may result in a less forgiving moral assessment. In the first case, the person "acts" and is liable; in the second, the person "omits" to act and is not liable. Of course, if a person takes on the responsibilities of a lifeguard, he or she is under a legal duty to act and an omission of this duty would become the basis of legal liability.

Similarly, the recognized duty of physicians to treat patients with appropriate technologies and methods means that criminal sanctions may be imposed on a physician whose patient died because of the physician's failure to act in circumstances under which no liability would attach for nonphysicians. The omission of a duty to take protective action by someone obligated to do so, such as a physician or a parent, is regarded by the law in the same way that an action would be that led to the same result.

Conclusion

Despite the fact that there are rather rigid and seemingly iron-clad prohibitions against intentionally taking the life of another, the administration of the criminal law allows a great deal of discretion, thereby permitting law to be tempered by justice, mercy—and even empathy. Reported criminal prosecutions of health care professionals for killing patients are almost non-existent. The major reason must be that such killings are rare; when they do occur, some may go undetected, and those that are detected are seldom prosecuted, perhaps because of the difficulty in obtaining a conviction.

Nevertheless, the threat of prosecution provides an appropriate protection against abuse. While "there is precious little precedent" one way or the other, as the Supreme Judicial Court of Massachusetts has observed, "what there is suggests that the doctor will be protected if he acts on a good faith judgment that is not grievously unreasonable by medical standards." Since neither wrongful shortening of life by physicians nor failure to give appropriate medical treatment for fear of the criminal law appears to be prevalent, society seems well served by retaining its criminal prohibition on killing, as interpreted and applied by reasonable members of the community in the form of prosecutors, judges, and jurors. Of course, in an era when medical and community standards are being reevaluated in light of changes in biomedical and sociocultural circumstances, some uncertainty about "reasonable medical standards" is inevitable. If the considerations and procedures suggested in this Report are taken into account, however, there appears to be no basis for concern that the law provides an inadequate or unsuitable framework within which practitioners, patients, and others can make decisions about life-sustaining care.

Suicide, or "self-killing," could be an issue with a dying patient either through an act or an omission of action. The common law treated suicide as a crime and punished both those who performed (or attempted) it and those who aided them. Though suicide is no longer punished as a felony, a suicide attempt—regardless of a person's motive—is a basis for active intervention by public officers and for deprivation of liberty (through involuntary psychiatric observation and treatment). Furthermore, a number of states continue to consider the assisting of suicide a crime.

NAZI LINKAGE TO EUTHANASIA—THE SLIPPERY SLOPE: POINTS AND COUNTERPOINTS

Andrew Scholberg vs. the President's Commission

The following counterpoints examine the "slippery slope" argument. This argument cautions against taking a first step that usually may be ethically justified but might lead to acceptance of other social actions that are not likewise justified. It is quite common for "slippery slope" arguments to use the Nazi movement in Germany as an example of how one step can lead to other steps that harm society. In the first statement below, Andrew Scholberg, writing in the Minnesota Daily, *uses this argument. The second statement from the President's Commission criticizes the logic of the "slippery slope" reasoning.*

Points to Consider

1. What arguments are made for and against the "slippery slope" reasoning?
2. Where were the first Nazi gas chambers constructed?
3. What kind of crimes took place in Nazi Germany?
4. Under what circumstances might a "slippery slope" argument have merit?

Excerpted from Andrew Scholberg, "Euthanasia: Death Without Mercy," **Minnesota Daily,** January 25, 1978 and **Deciding to Forego Life-Sustaining Treatment,** President's Commission for the Study of Ethical Problems in Medicine and Biomedical and Behavioral Research, March, 1983.

THE POINT
by Andrew Scholberg

The euthanasia mentality is a logical extension of the abortion mentality. The bond between euthanasia and abortion is most clearly seen in the context of amniocentesis, a prenatal diagnostic procedure in which amniotic fluid is drawn from a pregnant woman's uterus.

By analyzing the amniotic fluid, certain kinds of birth defects can be discovered—knowledge that prompts some couples to choose abortion. Aborting a defective child may correctly be called eugenic killing or prenatal euthanasia. Noteworthy is the fact that abortion and euthanasia are both expressly condemned by the Hippocratic Oath and by the World Medical Association's Declaration of Geneva.

An article in the "New England Journal of Medicine" in 1973 revealed that 43 defective babies had been "allowed to die" in Yale University's special-care nursery over a 30-month period. And Dr. C. Everett Koop, chief surgeon at Children's Hospital in Philadelphia, recently stated that "Children's Hospital is the only pediatric hospital in the country which neither permits abortion nor practices infanticide."

The euthanasia movement has been aptly labeled "the new annihilationism." Although euthanasia is not an uncommon practice, the fact that it is illegal is a deterrent for many physicians.

Not surprisingly, the annihilationists have been quite persistent in pushing for euthanasia legislation. For example, Dr. Walter Sackett, who has introduced so-called "death with dignity bills" in the Florida legislature every year since 1969, proclaims that "five billion dollars could be saved in the next half-century if the state's mongoloids were permitted merely to succumb to pneumonia."

Similar cost-benefit arguments were made in Nazi Germany regarding the crippled, the retarded and other "useless eaters," to use Hitler's phrase.

Nazi Germany

Nazi Germany is the only country in this century that has sanctioned euthanasia, a fact that the new annihilationists do not like to acknowledge. The euthanasia movement in Germany was inspired by a book published in Leipzig in 1920 entitled "The Release of the Destruction of Life Devoid of Value" by legal scholar Karl Binding and psychiatrist Alfred Hoche. Binding and Hoche argued that some lives are not worth living, that suicide is not intrinsically wrong, that it could not be a crime to help someone commit suicide, that some human beings are "devoid

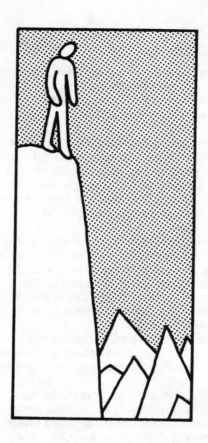

of value," and that killing "worthless people" should be legally permitted. Interestingly, these same arguments are being recycled by modern euthanasia enthusiasts.

In October of 1939 Hitler issued a letter authorizing mercy killing for the incurably sick. However, mercy killing soon proved to be a very slippery slope; victims of the Nazi euthanasia program included World War I amputees, unproductive old people, the mentally retarded, the mentally ill, bed wetters, children with "badly modeled ears," and others. About 275,000 defective people were killed.

The first Nazi gas chambers were constructed not at concentration camps but at mental hospitals; the gassings that eventually took place at Auschwitz and Maidanek were an outgrowth of the euthanasia program. Significantly, the German war criminals testified at Nuremburg that the ideas put forth in 1920 by Binding and Hoche inspired a substantial number of the killings that took place in the Nazi death factories.

58

So-called voluntary euthanasia bills frequently appear before state legislatures. Actually, proposals for "voluntary" euthanasia (assisted suicide) are a "come-on" to seduce the unwary into the euthanasia camp and to get "the camel's nose inside the tent . . ."

The Euthanasia Movement

Those who think that the euthanasia movement consists of just a few isolated lunatics are only kidding themselves. The influential California Medical Association, in an editorial in the Sept. 1970 issue of "California Medicine," stated that in the future "it will become necessary and acceptable to place relative rather than absolute values on such things as human lives . . ."

The editorial goes on to state that birth control and birth selection will be "extended inevitably to death selection and death control. . . ."

The fact that the annihilationists have already succeeded in bringing about massive, crass abortion in our society is an indication that they could achieve a similar victory for euthanasia.

The U.S. Supreme Court, in its Black Monday decision of Jan. 22, 1973, has already provided a rationale for permitting euthanasia by stating that some human beings, the unborn, are not "persons in the whole sense." Ominously, the Court did not specify that legal personhood begins at the moment of birth, thus leaving the door wide open for categorizing other classes of human beings—the newborn, the elderly, the handicapped—as nonpersons.

Citizens who believe in the intrinsic dignity and worth of all human beings must work to restore everyone's inalienable right to exist. As Edmund Burke once wrote, "All that is necessary for evil to triumph is for good men to do nothing."

THE COUNTERPOINT
by The President's Commission

An important concern regarding the potential of any policy to cause unintended harm is captured in the phrase "slippery slope." This argument cautions against taking a first step that is itself ethically justified when doing so is expected to lead to the acceptance of other actions that are not likewise justified. If the slope is indeed slippery and no likely stopping points exist to provide a toehold, then the wisest course may be to avoid taking the first step.

Slippery slope arguments are prominent whenever the protection of human life is at stake. Some people urge, for example, that intentional killing should be allowed if a person who will die very soon of an untreatable illness that is causing great and unrelievable suffering wants to die but is physically incapable of ending his or her own life. This position would clearly be opposed by people who hold that deliberate killing of an innocent person is always wrong. But it would also be opposed by those who might be willing to allow killing in such a situation but who fear that doing so would put society on a slippery slope because it would lead to killing in other, unjustifiable circumstances.

For such an argument to be persuasive, however, much more is needed than merely pointing out that allowing one kind of action (itself justified) could conceivably increase the tendency to allow another action (unjustified). Rather, it must be shown that pressures to allow the unjustified action will become so strong once the initial step is taken that the further steps are likely to occur. Since such evidence is commonly quite limited, slippery slope arguments are themselves subject to abuse in social and legal policy debate.

Slippery Slope Bogeyman

I guess the slippery slope must have been the Swiss philosopher's answer to the Arabic philosopher's camel's nose [under the tent]. . . . It seems to me that it is a bogeyman that is brought out in every discussion—again it's part of the hard-case problem. . . .

It then occurred to me that there was not a single problem that I was concerned about that didn't exist on a spectrum, and that any time you draw a line on any spectrum some fool can get up and point to the two things proximal to that line and say, "You mean, Dr. So-and-so, you think there's a difference between X and Y." And, of course, there isn't a difference between X and Y, because when you're on a spectrum, wherever you draw the line, you're going to find two proximal points that are almost identical. . . . You . . . [run the risk of going] all through your life never drawing a line.

Testimony of Dr. Willard Gaylin, transcript of 21st meeting of the President's Commission (June 10, 1982) at 144–45.

Obviously, slippery slope arguments must be very carefully employed lest they serve merely as an unthinking defense of the status quo. The cost of accepting such an argument is the continued prohibition of some conduct that is actually acceptable. Nevertheless, the Commission has found that in the area of concern of this Report, in which human life is at issue, valid concerns warrant being especially cautious before adopting any policy that weakens the protections against taking human life.

The Role of Law

Law is one of the basic means through which a society translates its values into policies and applies them to human conduct. Using the general rules embodied in statutes, regulations, and court decisions, society attempts judiciously to balance the degree to which various values may be pursued and to arbitrate situations in which serving one fully justified goal entails failing to serve another.

RECOGNIZING AUTHOR'S POINT OF VIEW

This activity may be used as an individualized study guide for students in libraries and resource centers or as a discussion catalyst in small group and classroom discussions.

Guidelines

Many readers do not make clear distinctions between descriptive articles that relate factual information and articles that express a point of view. Articles that express editorial commentary and analysis are featured in this publication. Examine the following statements. Then try to decide if any of these statements take a similar position to any readings in chapter two. Working as individuals or in small groups, try to match the point of view in each statement below with the most appropriate reading in chapter two. Mark the **appropriate reading number** in front of each statement. Mark (0) for any statement that cannot be associated with the point of view of any opinion in chapter two.

_____ **Statement one:** To assist in any way to bring about another's death is homicide.

_____ **Statement two:** The sanctity of life ethic requires that all life be treated with respect.

_____ **Statement three:** The quality of life must take precedence over mere physical survival.

_____ **Statement four:** The primary obligation of the medical profession is to preserve life.

_____ **Statement five:** Death with dignity is to be preferred over life which defaces one's humanity.

_____ **Statement six:** Society has a right to intervene in order to protect individuals from themselves even if the intervention is against their will.

_____ **Statement seven:** What we owe the sick is not help to die but help in dying.

_____ **Statement eight:** We are morally obligated to reduce pain and suffering in the world.

_____ **Statement nine:** There is no moral difference between allowing to die or accelerating death.

_____ **Statement ten:** Only God has the right to terminate life, since God is the author of it.

CHAPTER 3

LIVING WILLS: DEBATING THE ISSUE

NEW LAWS PROTECT TERMINAL PATIENTS

Stephen A. Wise

The following article by Stephen A. Wise appeared in
The Christian Century, *a journal of political and social
commentary. The author expresses support for legislation
he feels will protect the rights of terminally ill patients.
Some state laws now allow terminally ill patients to sign
"living wills" which proponents argue will protect
patients from receiving heroic medical treatment against
their wishes.*

Points to Consider

1. How does the author define the term "living will?"
2. What are the advantages of living wills?
3. Why do many people oppose living wills?
4. Why is legislation needed for living wills?

*Legislation permitting individuals to sign
binding, living wills requires nothing of them.
Rather it permits them to express explicitly
their prior wish for a natural end.*

When Ecclesiastes was written, it was safely pronounced that
"there is a time to be born and a time to die." But no more. Today science has developed sure and safe techniques of aborting
the beginning of life and of postponing death far beyond the
time when it would come naturally. Yet because both of these
techniques rest upon freedom of choice, and even though any
similarities stop there, dedicated right-to-life proponents vigor-
ously oppose legislation designed to protect terminally ill patients.

The resulting battle is a bitter mix of sometimes conflicting
ideas, for "the right to a natural death is one outstanding area in
which the disciplines of theology, medicine and law overlap."
Pressures on legislators can be enormous; emotions frequently
run high, and voting positions shift with volatility.

State Laws

Since 1976, 11 states have enacted statutes to assure patients
the right to refuse "heroic" measures that prolong dying. These
laws allow terminally ill patients to sign binding documents,
often called "living wills," in which heroic measures are refused
in advance; the patients are safeguarded in the manner of sign-
ing and revoking them; provision is made for objective medical
confirmation of the terminal condition; and the doctors, nurses
and health care facilities are given immunity for complying with
the patient's instructions.

Such immunity is critical, and other states have statutes in
process for granting it. The threat of lawsuits has increasingly
caused doctors and hospitals almost automatically to connect
patients to intensive-care, life-prolonging equipment—and then
to be terrified of disconnecting it. Three highly publicized cases
in the highest courts of New Jersey and New York illustrate the
problem.

Karen Ann Quinlan's parents finally obtained a court order to
disconnect her respirator because they were able to prove that
"before falling ill [into a vegetative coma] Karen had, on at least
three occasions, made explicit statements to the effect that were
she in a hopeless medical condition, she would not want her life
prolonged by the futile use of extraordinary medical measures."

Joseph Fox, an elderly member of the Society of Mary, was
also in such a coma, and a court order withdrawing his respira-

tor was obtained after the president of the society, Philip Eichner, proved his clearly stated wishes "not to have his life prolonged by medical means if there is no hope of recovery."

Simultaneously with the Eichner case, the same court rendered a different decision in relation to John Storar. In that situation, a terminally ill cancer patient was receiving large daily blood transfusions to keep him alive, but he had never had more than "a mental age of about 18 months." The court overruled his mother's objections to further transfusions because "it is unrealistic to attempt to determine whether he would want to continue potentially life-prolonging treatment if he were competent."

Thus the rule was spelled out: a terminally ill patient who is competent and who wishes to reject life-prolonging care may do so if his or her wishes are clearly expressed and proved. A Harris poll of public opinion in 1981 found that about 78 per cent of all people would prefer not to suffer pointless life-prolongation. The percentage was not significantly affected by differences in religious persuasion. However, except in the rare cases of prior written statements, the difficulty and enormous court costs of proving such wishes generally nullify them after a patient becomes incompetent.

The Opposition

A living will, carefully drawn, impartially witnessed, medically followed, and readily revocable, provides such proof and protects medical personnel and facilities. Various courts have indicated the need for legislative recognition of living wills. Yet vigorous opposition by "pro-life" groups in Connecticut has narrowly defeated such bills in 1979 and 1981, even though the 1981 bill was sponsored by several Catholic legislators.

That opposition does not have even the theological foundation and support which motivates the antiabortion movement, for both types of legislation are saying, "Let nature take its course."

On November 24, 1957, Pope Pius XII delivered a paper titled "The Prolongation of Life," in which he concluded that "the doctor in fact has no separate or independent right where the patient is concerned," that the patient's family is "bound only to the use of ordinary means" of care, that "the interruption of attempts at resuscitation is never more than an indirect cause of the cessation of life," and that, accordingly, a doctor may properly "remove the artificial respiration apparatus before the blood circulation has come to a complete stop."

On June 26, 1980, Pope John Paul II considered "the progress of medical science in recent years" and stated:

When inevitable death is imminent in spite of the means used, it is permitted in conscience to take the decision to refuse forms of treatment that would only secure a precarious and burdensome prolongation of life, so long as the normal care due to a sick person in similar cases is not interrupted.

Portions of that statement were even incorporated into the proposed Connecticut statute, although the separation of church and state prevented specific attribution. But the source was made well known to the legislators. Moreover, the legislators were told of the 1974 publication by the Catholic Hospital Association of a printed form, closely paralleling the proposed statute, stating: "If I can no longer take part in decisions concerning my own future and there is no reasonable expectation of my recovery from physical and mental disability, I request that no extraordinary means be used to prolong my life."

All these measures were to no avail. The opponents of the Connecticut bill increased their attacks. They asserted that it would legitimize euthanasia. They passed out fliers claiming that its passage would have permitted the death of such emergency cases as presidential press secretary James Brady. They delayed the bill until after midnight late in the session. They then argued emotionally without factual or theological basis . . .

Nevertheless, the bill will probably become law reasonably

A Hellish Nightmare

Technological advances have greatly increased modern medicine's ability to preserve and to save lives. Procedures which a decade ago were only dreams have now become a reality. However, like all human artifacts, sophisticated technology can be turned into an abuse; the very means used to preserve life may transform it into a hellish nightmare by reducing it to a sub-lethal extension of monitoring machines and sustaining apparatus.

John Paris, *America,* September 5, 1981

soon. Even formal diocesan opposition has waned, and the thinking of two popes and two prominent Catholic professors would seem to be persuasive. However, opponents of such legislation seem to be more emotional than rational.

A Natural End

Such opposition, if carried into the legislative trenches in the remaining 39 states, will inflict cruel and unusual punishment on terminally ill patients. It will deny them their right to meet their Maker according to their religious beliefs and in the manner and time of nature's choosing. It will go against the grain of human dignity in its final hour. It will mock both religious and secular pronouncements of the highest order: Pope John Paul II has said that "today it is very important to protect, at the moment of death, both the dignity of the human person and the Christian concept of life against a technological attitude that threatens to become an abuse." Thomas Jefferson poignantly observed that "bodily decay is gloomy in prospect, but of all human contemplations the most abhorrent is body without mind."

Legislation permitting individuals to sign binding, living wills requires nothing of them. Rather it permits them to express explicitly their prior wish for a natural end; it enables them to say, "There is a time to die with dignity," and it allows their own voices, not their doctor's and not the hum of an impersonal machine, to prevail.

68

LEGISLATION THAT COMPLICATES DYING

Thomas Horkan

The following statement is by Thomas Horkan, an attorney who testified on behalf of the Florida Conference before the President's Commission for the Study of Ethical Problems in Medicine and Biomedical and Behavioral Research. He opposes any legislation concerning the rights of dying patients and the living wills. His statement reflects reservations about government interference in the dying process.

Points to Consider

1. Why should the dying process be left unregulated by government?
2. What parties should be involved in the dying process?
3. What are the strengths and weaknesses of living wills?
4. Why is government legislation unnecessary?
5. What is the author's biggest reservation about legislation?

Excerpted from testimony by Thomas Horkan before the President's Commission for the Study of Ethical Problems in Medicine and Biomedical and Behavioral Research, 1981.

All the legislation that I have read, sets up a legislative process by which a doctor can or must withdraw extraordinary means from the patient. In doing that, it removes the family from that whole process.

I think there are some areas of life that are best left untouched and unregulated by government, and that is true whether it is legislation or judicial processes.

There are many areas of our lives like that, and I believe that the dying process and the medical treatment of dying patients is one of those areas.

People are all different. They die differently and they approach death differently.

Their families look at death differently. Their families have completely different relationships with the dying patient, and the families have their own problems.

Doctors themselves look at death differently. They practice medicine differently. They have different relationships with their patients generally, and by and large, they have different relationships or they will have a different relationship with a particular dying patient . . .

The Living Will

A living will can express the general thoughts that a patient has toward his subsequent medical treatment.

Generally speaking, it is executed without regard to what the medical problem is going to be. What is going to cause that person's death. Whether it be a lingering illness or sudden onset. Whether it be trauma or what-have-you.

There are many different ways that a person will be dying, and it also cannot predict, except when it is written during a terminal illness, it cannot predict when, at what stage of life that will be taking place.

So, we submit to you that the living will itself has problems.

It's a valid way to discuss with a doctor what your general intentions are, but when it is given legislative force or judicial force, then it becomes a mandatory document, perhaps after you have lost some degree of reason or perhaps after you have lost all reason at all.

American Medical Association

We feel that the legislation is not necessary. People die all over this country. They are dying every day, and by and large

70

those who have been put on life-preserving procedures, whether it be respirators or fibrillators or whatever it is, they have generally been put on those processes in order to restore health, in order to try to preserve the life while other attempts are being made to bring the person back to health.

When those measures fail, the vast majority of people are taken off of this machinery and permitted to die.

There's been testimony in Florida, and there's been a lot of writing on it. The American Medical Association has a policy statement on the matter, and that policy statement is one that by and large, I think, most physicians, most pastors and most religious groups concur in.

It basically says that the application or withdrawal of extraordinary means to prolong the life of a terminally ill patient should be the decision of the patient with his doctor or the patient's family with the doctor.

We feel that that basically is an ethical concept that is valid, and it is followed in this country today, and is the right approach to have, and mind you, it does not force anyone to do anything, but it sets up a process by which these decisions can be made.

Mandatory Action

The legislation, at least all the legislation that I have read, sets up a legislation process by which a doctor can or must withdraw extraordinary means from the patient. In doing that, it removes the family from that whole process.

It places in that physician the ultimate authority to decide how to follow the legislative mandate.

We feel that, or I feel that this kind of places into concrete, it projects the image that the physician is the master of the patient. Not that the physician is the servant of the patient, but

---

The Wedge Approach

We fear the "wedge" approach. As the "pregnant-by rape" argument was used to open the door to "abortion-on-demand," we rightfully fear that any breakdown, however small, in our traditional respect for the life of all human beings, may eventually result in policies of "genocide" toward the senile, or the retarded, or babies with severe defects.

Joseph D. Meissner at a National Right to Life Committee convention seminar.

---

rather that he is the master of the patient, and that the legislature has to come along and tell the physician under what circumstances he has to withdraw extraordinary means and under what circumstances he may withdraw those extraordinary means.

And, as I say, it removes the family from that process. When people die, it affects not just the person who is dying, it affects others, and in many cases it very imminently affects the family and has perhaps, a greater impact, if that could be possible, on the surviving family in some cases than the patient who may want to be released from this life.

That family has to go through a process of grief, and that process of grief should be starting during the dying process and they, I submit, should be involved in the decision-making.

For one thing, the family is often or usually a greater advocate for the dying person than is anyone else . . .

Biggest Concern

Lastly, one of the biggest concerns that we have is that for many years advocates of euthanasia programs, informative euthanasia programs, population programs, programs to eliminate the undesirable or the unproductive members of society have strongly advocated legislation to permit what they call "passive euthanasia," and we feel that passage of this legislation could well be the stepping stone to that type of legislation.

Our original opposition came with Dr. Sackett's legislation in which he very affirmatively and openly stated repeatedly, although he felt sometimes it hurt his cause, that this would permit the state of Florida to allow some 500 patients in Suniland Hospitals for the profoundly retarded to simply die by not treating infectious diseases or pneumonia, which he said were prevalent amongst the retarded.

He projected at that time a $5,000,000 a year savings to the state of Florida in this regard and, needless to say, that would engender enormous opposition, not only from us, but from advocates for the retarded and others.

We distrust this kind of legislation for that reason, and that distrust, if there were dire need for it, that distrust might be overcome, but we don't feel that there is any dire need for this legislation.

13 READING — DEBATING THE ISSUE

FOSTERING DEATH WITH DIGNITY

Society for the Right to Die

The Society for the Right to Die defines its goals and philosophy as follows:

The society believes that the basic rights of self-determination and of privacy include the right to control decisions relating to one's own medical care.

It opposes the use of medical procedures which serve to prolong the dying process needlessly, thereby causing unnecessary pain and suffering and loss of dignity. At the same time we support the use of medications and medical procedures which will provide comfort care to the dying.

It recognizes that a terminally ill patient may become unable to take part in medical care decisions and that a patient's previously expressed wishes may not be observed by physician and/or hospital.

It seeks to: 1) protect the rights of a dying patient, and 2) protect physicians, hospitals and health care providers from the threat of liability for complying with the mandated desires of those who wish to die with medical intervention limited to the provision of comfort care.

Points to Consider

1. What basic concept do living will laws recognize?
2. What specific similarities do these laws have in common?
3. How are the results of living will legislation described?
4. What is the most serious common deficiency in all state right-to-die laws?
5. Why are right-to-die cases decided in court so costly in financial and emotional terms?

Excerpted from the **Handbook of Enacted Laws,** Society for the Right to Die, 250 West 57th Street, New York, New York 10107.

The right to refuse treatment is a recognized legal principle, but the dying patient is frequently unable to exercise that right.

Medical capabilities to prolong life have increased dramatically in recent years. Artificially extending the lives of the terminally ill when there is no cure in sight can lead to a tragic confrontation between medical technology and the human needs of the dying patient.

Right-to-die laws are a much-needed response to this confrontation. Their intent is to establish and protect the individual's right to a dignified death without recourse to unnecessary, unwanted and undignified medical treatment which serves only to prolong dying and cause needless suffering. A second objective is to free physicians and other health care professionals from liability for honoring the patient's written directive.

These 'living will' laws are a new form of legislation. The earliest—the California Natural Death Act—was signed into law in 1976. Laws were passed in seven additional states in 1977: Arkansas, Idaho, Nevada, New Mexico, North Carolina, Oregon and Texas. Two more laws, in Kansas and Washington, were enacted in 1979.

The ten statutes are an extension of the individual's right of informed consent. The right to refuse treatment is a recognized legal principle, but the dying patient is frequently unable to exercise that right. Moreover, the problem is compounded when cessation of certain procedures will probably result in death. The implications of "pulling the plug" on terminally ill patients cause concern to even the most compassionate of doctors, especially if the patient is unable to communicate his or her wishes.

There has been a definite movement away from leaving treatment decisions solely in the hands of the physician. Fear of long agonizing dying has prompted thousands to protect themselves in advance by executing "Living Will" documents. Right-to-die laws give legal recognition to such documents.

Key Points of Laws

Each law presently enacted legally recognizes the right of a competent adult to refuse life-prolonging procedures if that adult is terminally ill. While not identical, they do contain certain basic similarities to provide necessary legal guidelines:

- Each provides the means for people to establish in advance that they do not want "heroic" measures used to prolong dying. This prior refusal is in the form of a written document, which must be signed and witnessed.

74

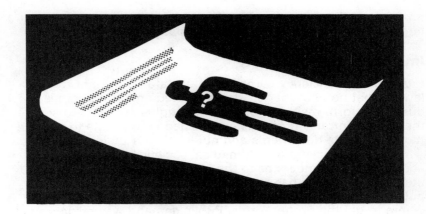

- The laws give immunity to the physician who acts in accordance with this document and to health professionals who act under the physician's direction.
- These laws require medical confirmation of the patient's terminal condition. Thus, while the patient's role is strengthened, the physician's role is not diminished. The laws make clear that it is the physician who has the competence to know whether the patient is in a hopeless and irreversible terminal condition.
- The patient's directive is binding upon the physician in all states except Nevada and North Carolina. However, in four states—California, Idaho, Oregon and Texas—the directive is binding only if it is executed or re-executed after the diagnosis of a terminal condition. (Even if the document is non-binding, it is important evidence to advise the physician of the patient's wishes. In addition, it provides legal immunity for the physician who acts in accordance with its directions.)

Results of Legislation

Experience with enacted legislation is significant, according to Sidney D. Rosoff, president of the Society for the Right to Die. "There has been no litigation as a result of legislation; fears of abuse have proved groundless. Overall, legislation has focused on appropriate and inappropriate application of medical technology; to clarify the rights of the terminally ill to refuse treatment; to set forth guidelines for physicians regarding the termination of life-support systems; to ease emotional anguish for families and physicians over whether heroic measures should be employed.

"Moreover, we have seen significant advances in improving

75

on California's pioneering law. The most recent statutes draw largely from the best of previous legislation.

Implementation of Laws

A striking deficiency common in all states with right-to-die laws is that none of the ten states created any formal procedures to inform residents of their new rights and how to secure them. No central source was established in any state to provide the appropriate documents and guidelines for their use.

Hospital associations and medical societies have sought to educate their members as to the implications of the new statutes, but the public has been left singularly uninformed. The public is either unaware that there is a law or it does not know where to get the proper forms. Public demand was evidenced by the response to a nationally syndicated "Dear Abby" column (August, 1980) telling readers about the ten states with "living will" laws. Following its publication, the Society for the Right to Die received some 30,000 requests for documents.

The Courts and the Dying Patient

Beginning in 1975, a number of right-to-die cases have been decided in the courts; the Quinlan case in New Jersey, the Saikewicz and Spring cases in Massachusetts, the Perlmutter case in Florida, the Brother Fox case in New York and the Severns case in Delaware. While opinions have generally upheld the right to have treatment terminated, the cases have not been distinguished by a speedy resolution of the issues.

The emotional cost to families of these protracted legal battles is inestimable. The financial costs can be measured. Father Philip Eichner, a petitioner in a New York court case brought on behalf of Brother Joseph Fox, an 83-year-old comatose patient being maintained on a respirator, asked: "Who can afford all these doctors, lawyers and court procedures which serve to put the average family in a bind?" Financial costs came to $87,000 in hospital bills for five months of intensive care to maintain the patient's vegetative existence and an additional $20,000 in legal fees.

When the Severns case had been in the Delaware courts for ten months, an editorial in a leading Delaware newspaper commented: ". . . the legal process is taking an emotional and financial toll . . . It is the absence of public policy on these matters which has placed the Severns case in the courts."

Most of the cases which have come before the courts have involved incompetent patients. The courts have been far from unanimous as to possible candidates to make end-of-life decisions on behalf of such patients. The list includes the attending

76

physician, the patient's next-of-kin or entire family, a hospital committee, the court, a court-appointed guardian and combinations of these decision-makers.

In the ten states where right-to-die legislation has been enacted the physician and family become instructed agents to follow the patient's prior directions. Their legal documents, executed while the declarant is competent, direct that the patient's wishes be honored by family and physician "in the absence of the ability to give directions regarding the use of life-sustaining procedures."

INVENTING LEGAL DEATH WARRANTS

Joseph P. Meissner

Joseph P. Meissner is a Cleveland attorney. A graduate of Harvard Law School, he has worked for many years in the areas of poverty law and civil rights. He has been a legal advisor to some fifty different community organizations, chairperson of the Cleveland West Side Community Mental Health Center, co-chairperson of Vietnamese Information Services which is a coalition of 12 different organizations active in the Resettlement Program, and President of the Right to Life Society of Greater Cleveland, Inc.

Points to Consider

1. How is a "living will" defined?
2. Why should a living will be called a death warrant?
3. What might lead to mercy-killing and what groups will be affected by mercy-killing?
4. Why could living wills become a "blank check" for physicians?

Joseph P. Meissner, "Euthanasia: A Legal Analysis of Death-With-Dignity Legislation," **Marriage and Family Newsletter,** March, 1978. Reprinted by permission of the publisher.

The "living will" is not directed toward living, but toward dying. Its purpose is to cut off life. Actually it should be labeled the "death warrant" because it authorizes the ending of the signer's life ...

A Living Will is a document which would be signed by an individual and which would give instructions to a physician caring for the individual during a critical illness. The document would provide for the ending of certain kinds of medical treatment and would be used when the patient's condition precluded communication with the physician. Allegedly, such documents would help in situations like that of Karen Ann Quinlan. While the idea sounds good, legalizing "Living Wills" will cause far more problems that it will cure ...

Introduction

Pro-life people have always predicted that euthanasia was the next logical step after abortion in attacking our civil right to life. The question has merely been what strategy would pro-death individuals and groups adopt in pushing for mercy-killing.

Already the outline of their strategy can be perceived. Death will become a right. In modern society "rights" are considered sacred. Group after group pursues their goals in terms of rights. "Right to privacy," "right to speak," "right to hearing," "right to a guaranteed annual income": these are only a few of the rights that fill today's headlines.

The mercy-killers are simply following in the historical paths of other groups by turning their goal of "death" into some innate right which everyone should be allowed to choose ...

Civil Libertarians

Unfortunately, today's civil libertarians offer little more wisdom to a troubled age than the hip phrase, "Do your own thing!" This union of "free choice" with the idea of controlling one's destiny even unto death is very appealing, particularly in an era which has lost much of its religious and spiritual foundations.

This explains why the Living Will has become the initial rallying cry for the mercy-killers. The term "living will" is a deadly misnomer. All wills are "living" since they are written by living people. Furthermore, the "living will" is not directed toward living, but toward dying. Its purpose is to cut off life. Actually it should be labeled the "death warrant" because it authorizes the ending of the signer's life ...

This Living Will is being pushed by an organization known as the "Society for the Right to Die, Inc." The name of this organization is as much a misnomer as the term "living will." The real rights at stake are the right to good medical care, the right to informed consent, and the right to compassionate care. Death, while the end of life, has never been considered life's goal. Even the Existentialists, such as Camus, who may deny all meaning to life and even contemplate suicide, still assert the value in man's struggle against the absurd and death. Furthermore, while death may be the outcome of various illnesses, there is no absolute certainty that death will follow any particular disease at any predetermined time. The term "right to death" is both confusing and misleading.

But even worse, such terminology leads inexorably to involuntary mercy-killing. How will this come about? Suppose "death" becomes a "right." Then anyone who desires death has a right to achieve this goal. In the beginning various conditions may be attached onto exercising this right just as there were restrictions initially on women obtaining abortions. But soon these limitations will be washed away just as happened to restrictions on abortions. Any distinctions between omissions or passive acts which result in death and positive actions leading to death will also be obscured. Meanwhile society will be confronted with the issue of what to do about those who cannot exercise and enjoy this new-found right to death.

Those in this deprived category would include the retarded, the babies born with defects, the senile, and all in various degrees of unconsciousness who did not make out a Living Will. In order to insure that these individuals did obtain their death benefits, guardianship procedures might be used. A general social attitude that no reasonable human being would want to stay alive under various conditions of handicap or disease could incline most guardians toward "pulling the plug." If this passive step did not result in death (such as in the Karen Quinlan case) or if the patient lingered on in a state of general misery (such as the Johns Hopkins' baby afflicted with Down's Syndrome,) guardians might be impelled to seek active steps which would hasten death such as by an injection or pill. If death is perceived as a desired benefit, then a guardian might even be required to take steps to insure that the ward can completely enjoy this final solution . . .

The World Scene

The right-to-die movement is not limited only to the United States. In Britain, a physician named Dr. John Goundry writing in the medical magazine **Pulse** states that doctors should be able to give the elderly a "demise pill" if they ask for it. "Society's

No Need To Legalize Death Wish

To our knowledge, no doctor in the U.S. has ever been indicted or successfully sued for *allowing* natural death to occur, i.e. discontinuing medication or artificial means of treatment of life support for a patient where such treatment has failed to cure the disease and who is in the process of dying. It is very unusual for a doctor to continue to "do everything" for such a dying patient today.

Never forget, the patient or/and family *can* always get another doctor if their present one, in their judgment, is not giving their loved one proper care.

Patients don't need the Death Wish (Living Will) made into law.

You are free to sign such a document now. Why freeze it into law?

J. E. Wilke, Past President, National Right To Life Committee, 1983

view of life," he predicts, "will change from the sentimental to the calculated and sophisticated and the overriding policy will be survival of the fittest." He even forecasts that the state will insist upon euthanasia for the elderly.

In Switzerland, voters in one state have approved a measure that would legalize mercy-killing. The plebiscite forces the state government of Zurich to initiate federal legislation to allow doctors to perform mercy-killings when requested by patients who are "suffering from an incurable, painful and definitely fatal disease." In Canada, members of an Anglican task force begin questioning the right to live of human beings with severe handicaps. Lorne Maeck, an M. P. P. for Owen Sound, has introduced a right-to-die bill in the Ontario legislature.

This recitation of anti-life incidents and articles could be extended easily for another twenty pages. The conclusion would remain the same. The Euthanasia Movement, whose public image was slightly tarnished after the Second World War, is now making an amazing comeback. The first step in legalizing mercy-killing is the promotion of Living Wills. Once the public has accepted the belief that certain lives are not worth preserving, the right-to-die benefit will be granted to all!

What Can Be Done?

If the above analysis is correct, then pro-life people must strongly oppose all efforts to legislate any kind of Living Will. In California certain pro-life groups, after initially opposing the Natural Death Act, became involved in the legislative game of compromise. When various minor changes and protections were added to the original bill, these groups withdrew their opposition. The poisonous fruit of this compromise can now be seen in the right-to-die legislation of other States as well as renewed agitation in California to "reform" its act. In many situations, goals of accommodation and "slicing the pie" are both necessary and ethical. But on the question of life, all of us should have learned a lesson from the continuing struggles against abortion. We can never compromise on the basic civil right to life of every human being, born or unborn, female or male, handicapped or healthy.

Blank Checks

Living Wills may become simply blank checks for physicians. This would be contrary to other legal developments. For example, laws now protect consumers and borrowers from entering hasty or uninformed transactions. Those charged with serious crimes must be read their rights before they can confess. How ironic it would be if the signer of a Living Will had less legal protection to informed consent than the purchaser of a used car . . .

If a patient signs a Living Will, he will have little chance to change his mind and thank a helping pro-life physician once the Will is carried out. Furthermore, if he signed it uder the stress and pain of an illness, is this really an exercise of free choice?

For this reason, many proponents support Wills signed before a serious sickness. But then the signer is not faced with the prospect of immediate death and so his choice may be more speculative than real. Living Will legislation attempts to meet this challenge by elaborate safeguards for revoking the directive. Yet these only accentuate the concern. Suppose the signer is unable to communicate during a later illness. He will draw little comfort from knowing he has a right to change his mind and revoke the Will.

Modern society, under the banner of freedom, has greatly enlarged the kinds and numbers of choices available to us. From what we eat to where we live, from where we work to who will be our leaders, today's world provides varied opportunities for us to make up our minds, and then change them, and then change them again. The Living Will tries to take advantage of our desires for choice. Yet if carried out, the Will—so far as humanly known—takes away forever our chance to choose.

82

THE LIVING WILL

This activity may be used as an individualized study guide for students in libraries and resource centers or as a discussion catalyst in small groups and classroom discussions.

Guidelines

The following document is a sample of a "Living Will" from the state of California. Read all seven points carefully. Then fill out the Living Will with information about yourself, your doctor, and preferred witnesses.

Then, working as individuals or in small groups, answer the following questions about your own living will. Choose the most appropriate number from sections 1, 2, 3 and 7 of the Living Will, where a choice is offered.

a. 1 2 3 7 I strongly agree with this statement. I would want my family and doctor to follow it closely.
b. 1 2 3 7 This statement is not very important to me. It does not reflect my values and desires.
c. 1 2 3 7 My family would have problems supporting me if I really wanted or believed this.
d. 1 2 3 7 The author of reading eleven would probably **most** agree with and emphasize this point.
e. 1 2 3 7 The author of reading twelve would probably disagree with this point more than the others.
f. 1 2 3 7 The author of reading thirteen would probably **most** agree with and emphasize this point.
g. 1 2 3 7 The author of reading fourteen would probably disagree with this point more than others.
h. I would/would not want to have and use a Living Will because

_____
_____
_____
_____.

A LIVING WILL

A directive to withhold treatment and for the administration of pain-killing drugs

To my family, my relatives, my friends, my physicians, my employers, and all others whom it may concern:

Directive made this _____day _____198____ I, _____ (name), being of sound mind, willfully, and voluntarily make known my desire that my life shall not be prolonged artificially under the circumstances set forth below, do hereby declare:

1. If at any time I should have an incurable injury, disease, illness or condition certified to be terminal by two medical doctors who have examined me, and where the application of life-sustaining procedures of any kind would serve only to prolong artificially the moment of my death, and where a medical doctor determines that my death is imminent, whether or not life-sustaining procedures are utilized, I direct that such procedures be withheld or withdrawn and that I be permitted to die naturally, and that I receive whatever quantity of whatever drugs may be required to keep me free of pain or distress even if the moment of death is hastened.

2. In the absence of my ability to give directions regarding the use of life-sustaining procedures, I hereby appoint

_____

(NAME) currently residing at _____, as my attorney in fact/proxy for the making of decisions relating to my health care in my place; and it is my intention that this appointment shall be honored by him/her, by my family, relatives, friends, physicians and lawyer as the final expression of my legal right to refuse medical or surgical treatment; and I accept the consequences of such a decision. I have duly executed a Durable Power of Attorney for health care decisions on this date.*

3. In the absence of my ability to give further directions regarding my treatment, including life-sustaining procedures, it is my intention that this directive shall be honoured by my family and physicians as the final expression of my legal right to refuse or accept medical and surgical treatment, and I accept the consequences of such refusal.

84

4. If I have been diagnosed as pregnant and that diagnosis is known to any interested person, this directive shall have no force during the course of my pregnancy.

5. I have been diagnosed, and notified at least 14 days ago, as being in a terminal condition by _____, M.D., whose address is _____ and whose telephone number is _____. I understand that if I have not filled in the physician's name and address it shall be presumed that I did not have a terminal condition when I made out this directive.**

6. This directive shall have no force and effect after five years from the date (above) of its execution, nor, if sooner, after revocation by me, either orally or in writing.

7. I understand the full importance of this directive and am emotionally and mentally competent to make this directive. No participant in the making of this directive or in its being carried into effect, whether it be a medical doctor, my spouse, a relative, friend or any other person shall be held responsible in any way, legally, professionally or socially, for complying with my directions.

Signed _____
City, County and State _____
of residence _____
_____
_____

The declarant has been known to me personally and I believe her/him to be of sound mind.

Witness _____
address _____
Witness _____
address _____

Footnotes:
*Under California law, for such an appointment to be as fully effective as the law will permit, it must be in the form of a "DURABLE POWER OF ATTORNEY FOR HEALTH CARE DECISIONS." Persons living in other states and executing this "Living Will" also might wish to execute that form (Durable Power of Attorney), as it might be honored by the courts of any particular state.

**If you are not a resident of California, strike out paragraph 5 in its entirety.

This directive complies in form with the Natural Death Act, California health and Safety Code, Section 9188.

CHAPTER 4

SAVING DEFECTIVE INFANTS: IDEAS IN CONFLICT

15

THE VALUE OF LIFE IS MOST IMPORTANT

Erma Craven

Erma Craven is the at-large Director of the National Right to Life Committee. Her article first appeared in the National Right to Life News. *The following statement is an abbreviated version that deals with the "Infant Doe" issue from the perspective of the National Right to Life Committee. Arguments are made that many deliberate killings of defective babies take place in America today.*

Points to Consider

1. What are liberals promoting in contemporary American society?
2. What is infanticide and why does it happen?
3. What point is made about abortion?
4. What happens when the value of human life is relative?

Erma Craven, "Infanticide: The Second Domino Falls," **NRL News**, December 7, 1981.

In America today, we are experiencing on an ever widening scale the deliberate killing of babies, not in the womb, but AFTER they are born, provided they are sufficiently "defective."

Few words ever galvanized the consciences of liberals quite like the opening sentences of the now-famous U.S. Advisory Commission on Civil Disturbances, popularly known as the Kerner Report. Established to probe the origins of the urban riots of the sixties, the Kerner Report prophetically warned that America was rapidly becoming two separate but unequal societies, one black, one white.

Aside from what this augured for future violence, what gave the Report its enormous impact was that this conclusion inverted one of our most cherished values: no longer could we assume that America is an upwardly mobile society, where one's status is achieved by effort, not ascribed by color.

Liberals were understandably horrified, partly out of guilt, but more, I suspect, out of a genuine disbelief that it had required the taking of human life, and the sacking of large sections of several cities to make Americans acknowledge the brutal realities of life in urban ghettos.

Yet less than fifteen years later, liberals are a major party to the establishment of an even more insidious division. It is a separation that transends color and is based on a cluster of ideas and assumptions completely at odds with the core values of our culture. It is based not on a visible stigma like color, but on an invisible stigma imputed to human beings—whether one is wanted or unwanted.

Lest this be taken as another special plea for the lives of the unborn let me say both yes and no. Yes, in the sense that I will never miss the opportunity to affirm the value of the lives of those who have yet to survive the temporary way station of the womb; but no, in that what I will examine here is promoting an ethic that, if accepted, will render the abortion debate obsolete. I refer to infanticide.

Deliberate Killing

While combatants on both sides of the abortion issue were busy debating the humanity of the unborn, ethicists(!), pediatricians and pediatric surgeons were quietly, inexorably carrying the logic of abortion one grisly step further. In America today, we are experiencing on an ever widening scale the deliberate killing of babies, not in the womb, but AFTER they are born, provided they are sufficiently "defective."

By David Seavey, USA TODAY

Understandably, this is not the kind of topic widely discussed. Indeed, it required one indictment and the publication of two interviews with parents who had deliberately killed their "defective" babies to strip away the layers of medical doublethink and hypocrisy that have served to hide the increasing acceptance of infanticide.

(Indeed, so difficult is this for anyone to believe, that until a few months ago, many prolifers scoffed at the warnings of one of their own, Surgeon General C. Everett Koop, that infanticide was becoming commonplace.)

Like all victims, before babies born with handicaps can be disposed of their humanity must be compromised. And, as always, this is accomplished through language. If we view these newborns as injured children, our first instinct is to care for and assist them.

But let that same infant be labeled "deformed," "abnormal," or "defective," and the burden is shifted to the helpless baby to prove why it should not be thrown onto the biological junkpile.

But just let someone whisper the incantation "choice" and liberals abruptly tuck away their feelings for the child and beat a hasty retreat to the higher ground of "respect for pluralism."

What jumps out at anyone who takes the time to read the published accounts of infanticide proponents is the world-weary pose they adopt which allows them to portray themselves as victims, forced to spend precious time defending their self-evidently correct ideas against the onslaught of prolifers and others irrationally committed to the medieval dogma of the absolute value of life.

The champions of infanticide (they prefer to say they want merely the "option" of infanticide, or as they call it, "benevolent euthanasia") go so far as to say it is cowardly to treat "mere biological life" with the same reverence one ascribes to Life (Capital L). In their Alice in Wonderland world, the truly courageous position becomes the refusal to let the tragedy of a "defective child" get in the way—and one does this by refusing to allow the necessary care to be administered.

Warming to the subject, proponents intimate that by withholding treatment, parents are grabbing Death by the lapels, so to speak, and spitting in His face. That it is the baby's life, not theirs', that is being sacrificed in this gritty act of defiance gets lost in the rush to void a biological mistake.

As a black woman, I know firsthand the absolute tyranny of slogans. I ask my fellow liberals, "Who pays for our miserable cowardice in the face of such question-begging, discussion-ending cliches as 'imposing morality'?"

For starters, there are the millions of unborn babies who can be aborted up until the day before their birth . . . if the mother so chooses. There are the children born with serious physical and mental handicaps who will not be treated . . . if their parents and doctors so choose. And there are the adolescent Down's Syndrome children like Phillip Becker, born with a fatal but correctible heart defect who can be denied life-saving surgery . . . if their parents so choose.

The scenario is depressingly familiar for one whose life-span covers history's bloodiest half-century. The justification is always the same. The victim flunks the criterion for Life (capital L) test as determined for him by his "superiors." In its mature form, this argument posits the insane notion that the victim's death is really for his own good.

90

Human Values

Where the value of human life is relative, just "one value among many," then one's value becomes "relative to expectancy of life, state of health, usefulness to society, or any other arbitrary criterion," as Rabbi Immanuel Jakobovitz has shown us.

As a life-long liberal Democrat, it grieves me that it is my liberal compatriots who have violated what should be the prime directive for any liberal: to defend the powerless and to uphold the dignity of every human life, regardless of age, color, sex, condition of dependency or physical handicap.

John Updike has observed in his novel **Couples** that "Death, once invited in, leaves his muddy bootprints everywhere." I fear that if we do not reinstate the "not for sale" sign on human life, it is only a matter of a very short time before the bargain basement sale of life comes into our house.

THE QUALITY OF LIFE IS MOST IMPORTANT

Peter Singer

Peter Singer teaches at the Center for Human Bioethics at the Monash University of Clayton, Victoria, Australia. The following article appeared in Pediatrics, *the official publication of the American Academy of Pediatrics. It does not, however, represent the official policy of the American Academy of Pediatrics.*

Points to Consider

1. What is the "sanctity of life view" and why is it under attack?
2. Why is the erosion of the "sanctity of life view" not an alarming event?
3. Why is human life not unique from other forms of life on the planet?
4. How are humans different?

Humans who bestow superior value on the lives of all human beings, solely because they are members of our own species, are judging along lines strikingly similar to those used by white racists who bestow superior value on the lives of other whites, merely because they are members of their own race.

The ethical outlook that holds human life to be sacronsanct—I shall call it the "sanctity-of-life view"—is under attack. The first major blow to the sanctity of life view was the spreading acceptance of abortion throughout the Western world. Supporters of the sanctity-of-life view have pointed out that some premature babies are less developed than some of the fetuses that are killed in late abortions. They add, very plausibly, that the location of fetus/infant—inside or outside the womb—cannot make a crucial difference to its moral status. Allowing abortions, especially these late abortions, therefore does seem to breach our defense of the allegedly universal sanctity of innocent human life.

A second blow to the sanctity-of-life view has been the revelation that it is standard practice in many major public hospitals to refrain from providing necessary life-saving treatment to certain patients. Although this practice applies to geriatric patients and those suffering from terminal illness, the most publicized and also the potentially most significant cases have been severely defective newborns. In Britain, Dr. John Lorber has quite candidly described his method of selecting which babies 'suffering from spina bifida should be given active treatment, and he has indicated, with equal candor, that in his view the best possible outcome for those not selected is an early death.

The decision not to treat an infant with Down's syndrome has also been publicized. In April 1982, in Bloomington, Indiana, the parents of an infant with Down's syndrome and in need of corrective surgery refused permission for the surgery to be performed. Few details are available because the court ordered the records sealed, but the court refused to intervene or to take the child out of his parents custody.

Although many doctors would sharply distinguish the active termination of life from a decision not to treat a patient for whom the foreseen outcome of this decision is the death of the patient, the distinction is a tenuous one, and the claim that it carries moral weight has been rejected by several academic philosophers. Hence, the acceptance of nontreatment in these situa-

93

tions is rightly perceived as a further threat to the sanctity-of-life view.

The Slippery Slope

Some respond to this situation with a sense of alarm at the erosion of our traditional ethical standards. We already have, these people tell us, one foot on the slippery slope that will lead to active euthanasia, then to the elimination of the mentally feeble and of the socially undesirable, and finally to all the atrocities of the Nazi era. To pull back from this abyss, we must renew our commitment to the most scrupulous respect tor all human life, irrespective of its quality . . .

Change Is Alarming

Is the erosion of the sanctity-of-life view really so alarming? Change is often, in itself, alarming, especially change in something that for centuries has been spoken of in such hushed tones that to question it is automatically to commit sacrilege. There is little evidence, however, to support the application of the slippery slope argument in this context. Cultures that have practiced forms of infanticide or euthanasia—Ancient Greece, the Eskimos—have been able to hold the line around those categories of beings that could be killed, so that the lives of other members of these societies were at least as well protected as the lives of citizens of the United States, where the culture officially accepts no limits to the sanctity of human life.

Whatever the future holds, it is likely to prove impossible to restore in full the sanctity-of-life view. The philosophical foundations of this view have been knocked asunder. We can no longer base our ethics on the idea that human beings are a special form of creation, made in the image of God, singled out from all other animals, and alone possessing an immortal soul. Our better understanding of our own nature has bridged the gulf that was once thought to lie between ourselves and other species, so why should we believe that the mere fact that a being is a member of the species Homo sapiens endows its life with some unique, almost infinite, value?

Humans and Animals

Once the religious mumbo-jumbo surrounding the term "human" has been stripped away, we may continue to see normal members of our species as possessing greater capacities of rationality, self-consciousness, communication, and so on, than members of any other species; but we will not regard as sacrosanct the life of each and every member of our species, no mat-

94

ter how limited its capacity for intelligent or even conscious life may be. If we compare a severely defective human infant with a nonhuman animal, a dog or a pig, for example, we will often find the nonhuman to have superior capacities, both actual and potential, for rationality, self-consciousness, communication, and anything else that can plausibly be considered morally significant. Only the fact that the defective infant is a member of the species Homo sapiens leads it to be treated differently from the dog or pig. Species membership alone, however, is not morally relevant. Humans who bestow superior value on the lives of all human beings, solely because they are members of our own species, are judging along lines strikingly similar to those used by white racists who bestow superior value on the lives of other whites, merely because they are members of their own race.

Ironically, the sanctity with which we endow all human life often works to the detriment of those unfortunate humans whose lives hold no prospect except suffering. A dog or a pig, dying slowly and painfully, will be mercifully released from its misery. A human being with inferior mental capabilities in similarly painful circumstances will have to endure its hopeless condition until the end—and may even have that end postponed by the latest advances in medicine.

The Human Difference

One difference between humans and other animals that is relevant irrespective of any defect is that humans have families who can intelligently take part in decisions about their offspring. This does not affect the intrinsic value of human life, but it often should affect our treatment of humans who are incapable of expressing their own wishes about the future. Any such effect will not, however, always be in the direction of prolonging life—as the wishes of the parents in the Bloomington case, and in several other recent court cases, illustrate.

If we put aside the obsolete and erroneous notion of the sanctity of all human life, we may start to look at human life as it really is: at the equality of life that each human being has or can achieve. Then it will be possible to approach these difficult questions of life and death with the ethical sensitivity that each case demands, rather than with the blindness to individual differences that is embodied in the Department of Health and Human Services' rigid instruction to disregard all handicaps when deciding whether to keep a child alive.

GOVERNMENT INTERVENTION AND INFANTS DOE: THE POINT

Marcia Angell

Marcia Angell is a medical doctor and is on the Committee on Publications of the Massachusetts Medical Society. This publications committee publishes The New England Journal of Medicine on a weekly basis. The following article deals with her reservations about federal government interventions into treatment decisions for seriously ill newborns.

Points to Consider

1. What were the "Baby Doe" rules?
2. What premise were they based on?
3. What are the two fundamental issues?
4. Who should decide what kind of treatment should be given to a seriously ill newborn?
5. What are the disadvantages of government intervention into decisions about medical treatment for seriously ill newborns?

Marcia Angell, M.D., "Handicapped Children: Baby Doe and Uncle Sam," **The New England Journal of Medicine,** September 15, 1983, pp. 659–61. Reprinted by permission of **The New England Journal of Medicine.** Vol. 309, pp. 659-661; 1983.

The efforts of the government might usefully be directed toward helping handicapped children reach their full potential and easing the hardship for them and their families. Instead they are expended on the inappropriate and damaging Baby Doe rules.

On July 5, 1983, the Department of Health and Human Services issued proposed rules to ensure that handicapped newborns, no matter how severe their handicaps, receive all possible life-sustaining treatment, unless imminent death is considered inevitable or the risks of treatment are prohibitive . . .

Baby Doe Rules

The Baby Doe rules are curious on a number of counts: (1) They were issued by an Administration that professes to abhor government regulations and has shown little involvement with the welfare of children in other settings. (2) They were promulgated despite formidable expert opposition—e.g., from the President's own Commission for the Study of Ethical Problems in Medicine and Biomedical and Behavioral Research and from members of the medical profession who actually live with these difficult problems . . . (3) They are based on the premise that all life, no matter how miserable, should be maintained if technically possible. (4) They attempt a remarkable distinction between medical decisions and decisions concerning the well-being of the patient, regarding the latter as outside the physician's purview but within the purview of the government. Oddly enough in this day of celebrating holistic medicine, the Administration thus seems to advocate that physicians not consider the whole patient, but rather act as highly skilled technicians whose job is to repair parts of the body. (5) They scarcely mention the parents of the handicapped infants, except to exclude them from decisions about life-sustaining treatment for their children. (6) They carry an adversarial tone that implies that handicapped newborns require protection from their parents and physicians.

Two Issues

It would be impossible to explore each of these issues here, but two of them are fundamental: Is the government correct in its judgment that the lives of all handicapped newborns should be maintained if technically possible? And is it proper for the state to substitute its judgment on such a matter for that of parents and physicians?

This certainly isn't an **invasion**, Mr. and Mrs. Doe. Think of it as a **rescue mission**.

BABY DOE

M.G. LORD, NEWSDAY

These are not easy questions. The government does have a legitimate interest in guarding the lives of its citizens and in protecting children from abuse and neglect. The state also has an interest in preventing systematic discrimination against classes of its citizens. However, these legitimate functions of the state have never before been used to mandate specific medical treatments for a large and extremely heterogeneous group of patients, on the premise that the quality of life has no bearing on medical decisions.

This is a dubious premise. It is in direct conflict with most current thinking about medical ethics, with the thrust of recent court decisions concerning life-sustaining treatment, and with the conclusions of the President's Commission in its report, Deciding to Forego Life-Sustaining Treatment. The right of a competent adult to refuse treatment is well established. Difficult court decisions have involved the rights of surrogates for incompetent patients to refuse life-sustaining treatment on their behalf. Even here, however, the goal of the courts has been to establish what the patient would wish if he were competent. The relevant point is that the possibility has been recognized that reasonable people might not want their lives prolonged in certain situations.

The variations in types and severity of handicaps in the newborn are enormous, and the government rules do not distinguish among them. Indeed, it is their intent that no distinctions be made. Thus, they prohibit ''any denial of benefits or services because of a handicap such as mental retardation, blindness, paralysis, deafness, or lack of limbs." Presumably, full life-sustaining treatment would be required for a newborn with all these handicaps together. The architects of these rules should think about that for a minute. Would a reasonable person wish to continue such an existence?

Strangely, the rules make no mention of the suffering of severely handicapped newborns. Instead they express the concern that a physician might decide that "a person is not worthy of treatment." This wording is mischievous in its implication. The issue in neonatal intensive-care units is not one of "worthiness," but one of future suffering. Do we have the right to inflict a life of suffering on a helpless newborn just because we have the technology to do so and despite the fact that we ourselves would have the legal right to reject such a life?

The second fundamental issue is whether judgments about the treatment of handicapped newborns ought to be made by the state. The usual intent of rules against discrimination is to protect individuals from malice or indifference. In the case of handicapped newborns, it is difficult to imagine people who are less malicious or indifferent than parents and physicians. Probably most parents would give their lives for their children; the circumstances in which parents would prefer death to survival for their child must be extraordinary indeed. For their part, physicians are accused of many wrongs in our society, but lack of therapeutic aggressiveness is seldom one of them. Indeed, physicians as a group are considered to be almost mindlessly devoted to keeping life going at all costs. Yet the Baby Doe rules seem to depict parents and physicians as adversaries of the infant who should be removed from decisions about whether to treat life-threatening disorders.

This is particularly cruel for parents, who are sometimes excluded by the medical establishment from participating in major decisions for their handicapped newborns and now face explicit exclusion by their government as well. Isolation and powerlessness of parents add to their suffering, as pointed out by the Stinsons in their book, The Long Dying of Baby Andrew.

Parents Should Decide

The President's Commission stated clearly that, unless there are strong reasons to the contrary in a given case, "parents should be surrogates for a seriously ill newborn." In making their decisions, parents should have access to advice from experienced physicians whose opinions reflect their total assessment of the individual case. For the government to think that it can do better with a set of general rules, which are of necessity insensi-

Government Interference

If the Reagan administration gets its way in the Baby Doe battle, we must give up one of the most important rights parents have: the right to care for their children without governmental interference.

Paul O. Sand, executive director of the National Conference of Christians and Jews, Upper Midwest Region, 1983.

tive and vague when applied to a particular patient, is both arrogant and foolish.

My objections to the Baby Doe rules should not be taken to mean that I think the earlier system of ad hoc decisions was perfect. It was not, and there could certainly have been instances of poor judgment by physicians and parents. (The case of Baby Doe may be one example; surely the idea of death by starvation is disquieting.) What should be done to prevent instances of poor judgment? Relman has suggested that when parents and physicians decide to withhold life-sustaining treatment, other physicians not involved in the case should be consulted and, if they concur with the decision, asked to so state in the patient's record. This is sensible and practical. When there are disagreements—between physicians, between physician and parents, or between the two parents—these should be discussed before an institutional committee. In all such discussions the presumption should be for life, with the onus of justifying their position placed on those advocating the withholding of treatment. Where private deliberations fail, the questions may be taken to court by any of the parties.

Handicapped infants salvaged in neonatal intensive-care units grow into handicapped children who often require more care and support than their families can provide. The numbers of these children are growing as the technology to save them improves. What happens to them? Institutional care for these children is sadly inadequate; it is fragmented and uncoordinated, not available to all who need it, and little more than custodial. Although this situation is not itself an argument against the Baby Doe rules, it does raise questions about the quality of our concern for handicapped children. The efforts of the government might usefully be directed toward helping handicapped children reach their full potential and easing the hardship for them and their families. Instead they are expended on the inappropriate and damaging Baby Doe rules.

GOVERNMENT INTERVENTION AND INFANTS DOE: THE COUNTERPOINT

John J. Conley

John J. Conley, S.J., is a student at the Weston School of Theology in Cambridge, Massachusetts. In the following article, he claims the debate over Baby Jane Doe has raised the wrong issues in the moral dilemmas of treating handicapped infants. He believes that the right-to-life vs. the right-to-privacy debate is not the proper approach in dealing with the complex social and moral dilemmas of seriously ill newborns.

Points to Consider

1. Who was Baby Jane Doe and what happened in her medical case?
2. Why was the decision to pursue conservative treatment for Jane Doe a correct one?
3. Under what circumstances is it not proper to withdraw treatment from a handicapped baby?
4. Why can government intervention into the treatment of handicapped infants sometimes be justified?
5. What is the central conflict in the Baby Jane Doe case?
6. How has the press distorted the issues?

John J. Conley, "Baby Jane Doe: The Ethical Issues," **America,** February 11, 1984, pp. 84–89. Reprinted with permission of the author.

If the proper medical care of a child is neglected, the state has every duty to intervene on the child's behalf, even against the guardian.

The case of Baby Jane Doe has provoked a complex debate in American society. It is a medical dispute on the proper care of a severely handicapped child and, analogously, all such children. It is a legal controversy on the respective responsibilities of parent, physician, hospital review board, child welfare authorities, state and Federal governments in the choices touching the life and health of a voiceless citizen. Most importantly, it is a debate on certain conflicting ethical values.

Typically, the conflict has surfaced in the American media as a conflict of "rights." The antagonists routinely stake their positions on the right to life, the right to privacy, the rights of parents, the rights of children, the rights of doctors in determining treatment, the rights of the handicapped and the rights of the local, state and Federal agencies to intervene when negligence or handicap discrimination is alleged.

The popular discussion of the case, however, has obscured some central ethical issues in our care for the handicapped human being in American society. There is a need to think through the thorny questions in the case from perspectives other than the right-to-life versus right-to-privacy arguments that have framed the very terms of public debate on the issue. The case raises fundamental issues about our obligations to the most marginal members of society (the child, the handicapped, the seriously ill) and about the responsibilities of the various social actors who declare these obligations.

Jane is a child of four months in a Long Island, New York, hospital. She suffers from multiple congenital defects: spina bifida (an open spinal column), hydrocephalus (excessive fluid on the brain), microcephaly (unusually small head) and malformation of the brain stem. Doctors advised her parents that Jane required spinal surgery or she would probably die at the age of two. The surgery, however, posed certain risks to Jane's health and life. Even if the surgery proved successful, Jane would probably remain bedridden, would suffer pain, would require constant medical care (including further possible operations) and would only live a maximum of 20 years. After numerous consultations, Jane's parents decided that this operation was not in Jane's best interests. With the doctors, they decided upon conservative medical care (nutrition, hygiene, antibiotic therapy) as the most appropriate treatment for Jane.

102

Risk and Benefit

The question here is what is the appropriate medical care for Jane Doe. A study of some analogous cases in determining the proper care for handicapped infants might illuminate the complex issues in the case.

Certainly, there are cases when handicapped infants are born in a "state of dying." Certain medical interventions (such as surgery) might prolong the dying for several months. In such a case, the child's guardian may well decide to forgo this medical intervention and simply rely upon more conservative medical care, since there is no hope of restoring the child's life or providing any benefit to the child (relief from pain, improvement in general health) by the intervention. Of course, this is precisely the sort of decision common in the care of any "normal" patient afflicted by a terminal disease. The patient (or guardian) may well refuse interventions that would only prolong the irreversible dying and that promise no benefit to the patient's health. In such cases, medical care focuses upon the comfort of the patient through routine care (hygiene, nutrition, treatment of pain and infection) as the patient dies. What is central here is that there is no discrimination in the treatment of patients according to whether they are "normal" or "handicapped." There is simply the choice of conservative medical care for patients in a particu-

lar situation: in an irreversible death process, where curative treatment has yielded to care focusing upon patient comfort. When such a patient is a child, the parents certainly have a primary role in the choice of the most appropriate treatment.

There are, however, other cases in which a handicapped person is denied proper medical care precisely because he or she is handicapped. Such was the 1982 case in Bloomington, Ind., where medical personnel permitted a child with Down's Syndrome to starve to death. At birth, the child had an internal blockage that prevented the intake of food. The parents refused to authorize the simple and routine operation to repair the blockage. A local court upheld their decision. The child subsequently died from starvation and dehydration. In the court testimony, the parents clearly argued that the refusal to operate was based upon the "kind of existence" a person with Down's Syndrome leads. Astonishingly, the doctors portrayed the life of a person with Down's Syndrome as a life of "idiocy." Yet such men and women are fully capable of language, self-awareness, human relations; and these are among the most rigorous "indicators of personhood." No one in the case denied that the surgery would have been performed on a "normal" child born with a similar blockage.

This was a terrifying act. The decision to refuse surgery and to allow the child to starve to death had nothing to do with the refusal of heroic means to preserve human life. It implied an eugenic double standard of health care, one for the "normal," another for the "handicapped." And the handicapped clearly enjoyed a standard that hastens their deaths and even inflicts pain. Such discrimination on the basis of handicap would appear to violate a number of state and Federal laws (especially the 1973 Federal Rehabilitation Act, which prohibits discrimination on the basis of handicap) and vitiates the constitutional guarantee to equal protection under the law. The unusually callous nature of this child's death (from progressive starvation) only underscores the tragedy of this decision.

But what of the case of Jane Doe . . .

Distortions of the Ethical Issues

The media's presentation of the choice of conservative medical care for Jane, however, rarely focuses upon the precise medical grounds that render the choice, in this specific case, a reasonable one. The accounts tend to justify the choice in a loose quality-of-life discussion. The general argument often runs as follows: Jane's handicapped life is intolerably tragic. She would be bedridden. She would be severely retarded. She would not really be a person. She could not have a "meaningful" life. She would be a burden, to herself, to her family, to society at large,

104

which must care for such severely retarded citizens. According to this argument, one should permit Jane to die because she would lead such a severely handicapped life. Few would argue that one could actively take her life as an act of mercy. Most would simply argue that one should give her minimal care and allow her to die at the earliest possible date. By refusing the life-prolonging surgery, the parents are sparing Jane, themselves and the rest of society the burden of a tragically handicapped life . . .

The media have also distorted the case by arguing that the fundamental issue is the right to privacy (of the parent and physician) in the treatment of sick children. Certainly the parents have a primary role in the choice of medical care for their children. Similarly, the attending physician has a prime responsibility in the diagnosis of the child's illness and the determination of appropriate therapies for dealing with the illness. And in cases as complex as Jane Doe's, private hospital review boards can be helpful in clarifying all such choices in the light of general medical principles and the wisdom gleaned from analogous cases. Such parental and physician discretion, however, is hardly absolute. Children are not the property of parents and physicians. State agencies routinely intervene on a child's behalf when abuse or neglect (including the neglect of proper medical care) is alleged. Discrimination on the basis of handicap violates a number of state and Federal laws. Parental discretion in the medical care of children cannot be used to veil the violation of laws that protect human life, guide medical practice, protect the handicapped from discrimination and anchor the right of every citizen to equal protection under the law . . .

If the proper medical care of a child is neglected, the state has every duty to intervene on the child's behalf, even against the guardian. If guardians and/or doctors should discriminate against someone on the basis of handicap, the government has clear grounds for vigorous intervention. The Jane Doe case simply offers little convincing evidence of such negligence or discrimination in the choice of conservative medical treatment.

A Model of Ethical Legal Analysis

Judge Leonard Wexler provides the clearest analysis of the issues in the Jane Doe case in his opinion denying the request of the Justice Department to have access to Jane's medical records. The Judge argued: "The decision of the parents to refuse the consent to the surgical procedures was a reasonable one based on the medical options available and on a genuine concern for the best interests of the child". . .

He ruled that the hospital's course of treatment and the parents' choice regarding that treatment did not discriminate against the handicapped. The Government's suspicions in this case seemed poorly founded, given the repeated examinations in the public forum . . .

Judge Wexler's opinion clearly supports the rights of Government to intervene on the child's behalf when abuse, neglect or discrimination is alleged. He criticizes too absolute a concept of privacy (either of the parent or of doctor-patient confidentiality) that could easily veil the mistreatment of handicapped children. In this particular case, the allegations of such neglect or discrimination are simply unconvincing.

Judge Wexler's opinion narrowly justifies the conservative medical care of Jane as a reasonable choice, given the risky options. The foundation is not a patient's, parent's or doctor's right to privacy. The justification is not any argument that Jane's tragic quality of life merits her less medical care or legal protection than anyone else. The decision firmly analyzes the choice of medical care in the light of certain universal medical and legal principles. The refusal of such risky surgery is a reasonable choice for any patient (or guardian) according to the norms of medical practice. The plan of conservative care promises to benefit Jane in certain ways (especially in treating infections), thus qualifying as "beneficent treatment" for a patient in admittedly dire circumstances. Further, the proper treatment of Jane Doe (and all such children) is a question of public concern, not a matter of private concern confined to the family and the doctors. The interventions of local agencies to investigate allegations of negligence and of the courts to investigate allegations of discrimination are perfectly legitimate . . .

The Handicapped in Contemporary Society

The popular discussion of the Jane Doe case raises some disturbing questions on contemporary attitudes toward the handicapped. The reduction of the complex issues to a single question of "privacy" threatens the fundamental rights of the handicapped citizen. The proper care of the handicapped child is a social and legal concern, a proper domain for the legislatures, the courts and government agencies. It is not a purely private affair, confined to the discretion of parent and physician. The defense and promotion of the fundamental rights of every citizen (such as the right to equal legal protection, to life and to reasonable medical care) is the very rationale for constitutional government.

The defense of children's rights (such as the right to proper health care when parents are negligent) occasionally requires state intervention against parents "in the privacy of the home." The state has every duty to promote the welfare of its handicapped citizens through legislation against discrimination, through economic assistance to the handicapped and those who care for them, through state-supported hospitals and group homes and through sound special education and care programs. Obviously, there is a danger in a paternalistic government that supplants the family and physicians in every thorny health-care dilemma. But there is far greater danger in a society that reneges on its legal, medical and economic duties to its most powerless members (the infant, the sick, the handicapped) under a veil of privacy.

BETWEEN THE EXTREMES: A RATIONAL COMPROMISE

Don Nickles

Don Nickles is a United States Republican Senator from Oklahoma. The following statement before the United States Senate supports an amendment to the Child Abuse Prevention, and Adoption Reform Act. Part of the amendment which Senator Nickles helped to write deals with the treatment of seriously ill newborns.

Points to Consider

1. Why is the amendment referred to as a middle-ground approach?
2. What groups support the amendment?
3. What specifically does the amendment require and not require?
4. What is your opinion of the amendment?

Senator Don Nickles, **Congressional Record,** July 26, 1983, pp. 9324–25.

The last new provision of this package is an amendment which Senators Hatch, Denton, Kassebaum, Cranston, Dodd, and I have offered to S. 1003 to deal with the so-called "Baby Doe" issue. The amendment expands the responsibilities of State child protective service agencies receiving Federal funds under this program to include procedures and/or programs for responding to reports of medical neglect, including the alleged denial of necessary medical treatment for handicapped newborns. In reality, this is not a new responsibility in most States since the child abuse statutes could be interpreted to include this form of medical neglect.

It is an understatement to say that defining what constitutes medical neglect is fraught with difficulties, sensitivities, and very fine lines. No one wants Washington establishing medical standards and practices for every case or diagnosis. Yet, on the other side of the equation, no one wants to condone the discriminate denial of medical treatment for infants simply because they may suffer some degree of retardation, paralysis, or other disability. Our Nation has come too far in the mainstreaming of persons with disabilities into all aspects of society to sanction a quality of life ethic in which only those who are fit or productive or functioning members of society are allowed to live. I believe that this legislation represents the best middle-ground approach to the issue.

The Provisions

First, it designates States, rather than the Federal Government as the first tier of review for any allegation of the withholding of medically indicated treatment from an infant. The State child protection authorities are encouraged to establish a working relationship with hospitals, particularly those which serve as referral centers for children born with complications, not only for purposes of any neglect reporting, but also for the exchange of information about what services are available to an infant born with disabilities and his or her family. One of the most helpful things for a family dealing with the trauma of the birth of a handicapped child is to talk with other parents who have gone through the same experience. The Rossaw family of Connecticut have adopted 11 children with various disabilities. In their experience, this single recommendation is the one which has made the most difference to families coping with an unanticipated complication at birth. I envision that the child protective services can serve as a conduit for this kind of exchange and for notification of the other services which may be available in the community.

Second, the amendment to S. 1003 provides a carefully

crafted definition of the phrase "withholding of medically indicated treatment" to guide States in carrying out the provisions of this act. This language was the product of a broad spectrum of interests from the medical, hospital, disability, and prolife organizations.

The Supporters

Those who now support it include: The American Hospital Association, the Catholic Health Association, the American Academy of Pediatrics, the American College of Obstetricians and Gynecologists, the American Nurses Association, the American College of Physicians, the National Association of Children's Hospitals and Related Institutions, the California Association of Children's Hospitals, the Nurses Association of the American College of Obstetricians and Gynecologists, the American Association on Mental Deficiency, the Association for Retarded Citizens, U.S.; the Spina Bifida Association of America, the Down's Syndrome Congress, the Association for Persons with Severe Handicaps, the Disability Rights Center, People First of Nebraska, Operation Real Rights, the National Right to Life, and the Christian Action Council.

Withholding of medically indicated treatment is defined as: the failure to respond to the infant's life-threatening conditions by providing treatment (including appropriate nutrition, hydration, and medication) which, in the treating physicians' or physician's reasonable medical judgment, will be most likely to be effective in ameliorating or correcting all such conditions, except that the term does not include the failure to provide treatment (other than appropriate nutrition, hydration, or medication) to an infant when, in the treating physicians' reasonable medical judgment, (A) the infant is chronically and irreversibly comatose, (B) the provision of such treatment would not be effective in ameliorating or correcting all of the infant's life-threatening conditions, (C) the provision of such treatment would merely prolong dying, or, (D) the provision of such treatment would be almost entirely futile in terms of the survival of the infant and the treatment itself under such circumstances would be inhumane.

I think that this language is very clear in what it does not require. First, it does not require unending treatment of an infant which is doomed to die regardless of what is done. If the child is born dying, then only that which is necessary to feed the child and relieve pain is required. Second, if a child is born with more than one anomaly, and one or several are correctable with treatment, but the child has some condition which is fatal and untreatable, then the physician is not being mandated to take the infant through repeated surgeries for the correctable conditions). Third, the language does not apply to children in comas.

110

Finally, the last exception allows for the so-called gray areas. These are the cases when the child has a very slim chance for survival and the physician must make a judgment call as to whether the odds of correcting the child's condition are strong enough to merit an attempt to save the baby, even with treatment that may be very painful. This provision in our language gives a physician the leeway needed to make such a judgment call without fear of violating the letter or spirit of this legislation.

What Is Required

What does this language require, then? It requires a physician to treat treatable medical conditions to the best of his/her ability without regard for any handicap that a child may have. For example, a child born with Down's syndrome who also has an esophagus which needs surgery cannot be denied that surgery and allowed to die simply because he or she will suffer some unknown degree of retardation. Or, a child born with spina bifida cannot be denied aggressive life saving treatment simply because he or she may need leg braces to walk.

Cathryn Donnelly of Tulsa, OK, was born with spina bifida. No one could have predicted how Cathryn's family would handle her disability, how she would cope, what the degree of her paralysis would be, or if she would suffer any mental impairment. Yet, there are decisions being made in hospitals today which judge all of these things in the first few days of birth and rule against treatment because some alleged quality of life is not expected. I am not comfortable setting standards for who shall live and who shall die, nor am I comfortable allowing someone else to make such a decision for me. The standard that has been part of our common law is to treat those for which there is a reasonable chance to save, regardless of whether or not they are going to be retarded, paralyzed, or otherwise disabled. Obviously, such a standard requires that we, as a society, are willing to commit the resources necessary to help this population reach their potential. We have gone a long way at the Federal level to try and ensure that medical, rehabilitative, educational, and other services are available to meet that commitment.

In closing, I would like to say that this compromise in the "Infant Doe area is one that is a reasonable balance between the twin objectives of minimal Government interference, while ensuring adequate protection regardless of age, handicap, sex, or race.

INTERPRETING
EDITORIAL CARTOONS

This activity may be used as an individualized study guide for students in libraries and resource centers or as a discussion catalyst in small group and classroom discussions.

Although cartoons are usually humorous, the main intent of most political cartoonists is not to entertain. Cartoons express serious social comment about important issues. Using graphic and visual arts, the cartoonist expresses opinions and attitudes. By employing an entertaining and often light-hearted visual format, cartoonists may have as much or more impact on national and world issues as editorial and syndicated columnists.

By David Seavey, USA TODAY

Points to Consider

1. Examine the two cartoons in this activity.

2. How would you describe the message of each cartoon? Try to describe each message in one to three sentences.

3. Do you agree with the message expressed in either cartoon? Why or why not?

4. Are any of the readings in chapter four in basic agreement with either of the cartoons?

5. Which reading in chapter three would be in basic agreement with the message of either cartoon?

By David Seavey, USA TODAY

CHAPTER 5

ORGAN TRANSPLANTS AND HIGH-TECH MEDICINE: PRO AND CON

TRANSPLANTS SAVE LIVES AND MONEY

Norman Shumway and G. Melville Williams

Norman Shumway is a medical doctor and professor of surgery at the Stanford University School of Medicine, Stanford, California. Dr. G. Melville Williams is a professor of surgery at Johns Hopkins Hospital and president of the American Society of Transplant Surgeons. In the following congressional testimony they relate how organ transplants save lives and financial cost.

Points to Consider

1. How widespread is the heart transplant procedure?
2. How effective are heart transplants?
3. How effective have kidney transplants been?
4. What can be done to contain the costs of kidney transplants?

Norman Shumway and G. Melville Williams in testimony before the House Subcommittee on Investigations and Oversight, 1983.

Transplantation of the heart is a proven therapeutic intervention with a 5-year survival of at least 50 percent, and 1-year survival rate that approaches 80 percent.

Testimony of Dr. Norman Shumway

I speak for the entire panel that we are grateful for this opportunity to say a few things about the transplantation of tissues in each of our particular specialties.

First, let me make a few general comments regarding the present status of heart and heart-lung transplantation. I would like then to focus on the somewhat special problems associated with heart and heart-lung donors.

During the last decade, tremendous progress has been made in the science and practice of transplantation. New drugs have become available to control more effectively the immune response to transplanted tissues. As a matter of fact, since we began the use of cyclosporine A in December 1980, there has not been a single instance of clinically diagnosable rejection of the allografted heart. In other words, no patient has shown any signs of cardiac failure as a result of the transplanted tissue.

The developing technology for organ preservation has widened the pool of donors. Hearts can now be transported probably up to 2,000 miles with every expectation that the transplant will perform satisfactorily immediately. Further work is progressing nicely in this area of research, and the day will come when hearts can be preserved to the same temporal limits enjoyed now by renal and liver grafts.

Last year, in the United States, alone, approximately 100 patients underwent cardiac transplantation, 30 at Stanford. The 1-year survival rate now stands at 80 percent, and fully 90 percent of all patients having heart transplants at Stanford leave the hospital in stable condition. This statistic contrasts markedly with the 22 percent 1-year survival 15 years ago, which was the first year of clinical heart transplantation at Stanford University.

Of 260 patients having cardiac transplants, 106 at Stanford are alive and well now between 13½ years and 2 weeks following the procedure. Suffice it to say that transplantation of the heart is now on the same therapeutic footing as kidney transplants. Medical centers all over the world are re-entering the field, and many clinics are producing results comparable to our own. This year, the number of transplants should at least double last year's total with further expansion to be expected later in the decade.

The hospital cost for a patient having heart transplantation at

116

Stanford is roughly twice that for a standard open heart surgical procedure at Stanford. No professional fees have ever been charged for any transplantation procedure, either heart or heart-lung. Donor costs average $3,000 and are independent of whether the donor is an on-site donor or in another hospital.

Recent Progress

In the past, transplantation of the lungs has produced the most dismal results of any kind of organ transplantation. Of 38 unilateral lung transplants, no patient lived as long as 10 months, and most patients died within a few days to a few weeks after the procedure. Presently at Stanford, 8 of 11 patients having transplantation of both lungs along with the heart are alive and well, out of the hospital and fully rehabilitated 2 months to 2 years after the transplant.

Irrespective of any conceivable advance in artificial organs, heart-lung transplantation is here to stay. The concept of a totally implantable artificial heart with an inexhaustible, noiseless, nonheat-producing energy source is one that we all respect, but its realization is decades away. The early clinical results of heart-lung transplantation at Stanford are so gratifying that other centers are almost certain to develop their own programs. Twenty-one such transplants have now been done worldwide, and next year we will see perhaps another fifty . . .

In summary, then, transplantation of the heart is a proven

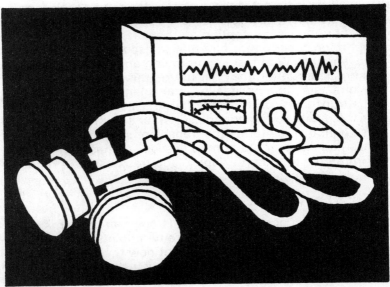

therapeutic intervention with a 5-year survival of at least 50 percent, and 1-year survival rate that approaches 80 percent. Physicians taking care of brain-dead individuals and the families of brain-dead patients are becoming increasingly aware of the need for transplantable organs. Additional programs are being inaugurated to train health care personnel in the maintenance of various organs in transplantable condition.

While there may be some future application for the artificial heart as an interim device before transplantation, there is no such mechanical substitute for the lungs, and the early results of transplantation of the heart along with both lungs are even better than for transplantation of the heart alone. So it is clear that the need for adequate identification and care of donors is of tremendous and ever-increasing importance.

Kidney Transplants—Testimony of Dr. Melville Williams

It is possible to summarize national efforts in kidney transplantation using round numbers as follows: somewhat more than 5,000 kidney transplants are performed per year; of these, 30% of the kidneys come from related living donors; 3,300 kidneys can be expected to provide life sustaining function; 2,500 individuals may be expected to return to work or to premorbid social activity; and 500 individuals die . . .

In the past there has been concern that some patients with kidney failure were denied access to the transplantation system. Virtually all patients enter the system after having their lives sustained by dialysis. Thus, referral to a transplant center is entirely dependent upon the perception on the part of the patient and the nephrologist caring for him that transplantation offers distinct advantages. With results improving and with the prospect of real breakthrough in the near future, this problem, I believe, will be diffused. Patients awaiting transplantation are registered with the transplant center and undergo tissue typing and screening for the presence of antibodies in their serum. The presence of these antibodies informs the transplant surgeon that the patient has had exposure to human tissues and has developed some immunity to them through blood transfusions, pregnancies, or other transplants . . .

The Cost Factor

The problem of cost containment is one that concerns many of us in transplantation and there are two points to be made. First, there is a widespread notion that new therapy is costly therapy. Regrettably, this is true in many instances, but in many others it is quite short-sighted. For example, there was a recent directive from the Health Care Financing Administration that it would not pay for purposeful blood transfusions in the living donor situation described. The charge for drawing a unit of blood and dividing it into thirds for subsequent transfusion is one-third the charge of one dialysis treatment and the result may be a 90% successful outcome of the transplant. Support must be given to agencies such as the Office of Technology Assessment to develop a reasoned approach in the application and evaluation of new methods of therapy and means of reimbursement in the field of transplantation. The second point regarding cost and transplantation is that in purely economic terms, long term disability associated with expensive therapy costs more than death which costs much more than a cure. One can do some rather simple calculations regarding the expenditures required to sustain a disabled individual on hemodialysis. We, the taxpayers, pay for the medical therapy and the social security benefits accrued to the individual. We also lose taxes from the loss of income. In the event of death, we are faced with paying social security death benefits and we lose income from taxes. In the case of cure, we pay for the medical therapy but recover money from taxes.

The only way costs can be substantially reduced is by increasing the number of transplants performed.

THE COSTS ARE PROHIBITIVE

George Crile, Jr.

Dr. George Crile is a surgeon and the former head of the department of general surgery at the Cleveland Clinic in Cleveland, Ohio. In the following article he questions large investments in very costly organ transplants and other high-technology medical techniques. He believes society may be better served by less costly research and programs to prevent disease and promote healthy habits and behavior.

Points to Consider

1. In what ways have the costs of medical treatment increased?
2. What kind of new medical procedures have been developed?
3. What criticisms does the author make toward organ transplants and high cost medicine?
4. What alternative does he suggest to continued investment and research in high-technology medicine?

George Crile, Jr., "Modern Miracles: Can We Afford High-Tech Medicine?" **The Washington Post,** 1983. Reprinted with permission of the author.

120

One thing is certain: We cannot anticipate an average life span of more than 100 years even if all diseases become curable.

We live in an era of exploding medical costs but diminishing medical returns. We are spending huge sums on health care—now more than 10 percent of our entire gross national product—but we are getting less for the money than in times past.

Most of the striking increase in the life expectancy of Americans came between 1900 and 1960. This was the period in which vaccination, public health and hygiene became standardized, and, in the latter part of the period, when antibiotics were introduced. In each 20 years of this period, the life expectancy of the average American increased by seven to eight years.

But in the 20 years since then, 1960 to 1980—a period in which the capabilities of medical technology, the use of surgery and the cost of medical care have unprecedentedly skyrocketed—the increase in life expectancy rose only 3.3 years, to 73.3. These figures suggest that the law of diminishing returns is beginning to operate.

What, then, can we forecast for the cost-effectiveness of medical care in the future?

Advanced Technology

Twenty years ago, if you had a pain in your abdomen, you would have had a physical examination, X-rays of the gastrointestinal tract, blood tests and a urinalysis. Today, in addition to those tests, you would have a CAT (Computerized Axial Tomography) scan (cost: $250–$500) or a scan by a Nuclear Magnetic Resonator (estimated cost: $400). And for what benefits? Perhaps to find an incurable cancer of the pancreas. Also, according to an April article in The New England Journal of Medicine, "over-reliance on these new procedures occasionally contributed directly to missed major diagnoses."

In addition to the scans, you would also be apt to have an examination of the stomach and duodenum with a flexible endoscope that can be passed from the mouth all the way to the large intestine ($150 to $1,000). Then, for only $80 more, there would be an ultrasound examination of the gallbladder and liver in search of gallstones.

CAT scanners are only the beginning. Consider the PET (Positive Emission Tomography) scanners that are already operating in a half-dozen medical centers and are planned for as many more. They may make revolutionary changes in the diagnosis of some types of heart disease and cancers and in most diseases of the brain, including the incurable Alzheimer's disease

121

and various psychoses. They even show what part of the brain is being used when you move or think. They indicate the location and extent of chemical activity.

There is only one problem with the futuristic dreams that the PET scanners evoke, and that is the scanner must be located next to a cyclotron. A cyclotron costs $2 million to $3 million, plus $1,000 an hour to run. A PET scanner costs $1 million. As a result, we will have a $3 million to $4 million investment in a machine that can perform only three or four scans in a day.

I leave it to you to estimate what the cost of a single PET scan will be. One authority has put it at $8,000. The scan would not be very cost-effective if all it showed was that your loss of memory was due to the incurable Alzheimer's disease.

Threat of Litigation

One of the major factors in the cost of medical care is the ever-increasing incidence of malpractice suits. I know a plastic surgeon in Los Angeles who pays $85,000 a year in malpractice insurance. If he does 425 operations a year, that means he pays his insurance company $200 for each operation before he even picks up his scalpel. Who pays this $200? Ultimately, the patients do, through the increased cost of medical insurance.

The threat of litigation also forces physicians to practice defensive medicine, which means ordering every test known, so that if the patient sues, his lawyer cannot accuse the physician of negligence. Moreover, it often results in the performance of unnecessary operations, because somehow, in the eyes of a jury, the surgeon who loses a patient as a result of an unnecessary operation doesn't seem as negligent as one who loses a patient because he did not operate at all.

For example, more than $50 million was awarded recently to the parents of a child who suffered brain damage in a complicated delivery that the lawyers claimed could have been avoided if a Caesarean section had been performed. Small wonder that in many areas nearly a third of our babies now are being born by Caesarean . . .

Artificial Organs

Before the 1950s, kidney failure spelled death. Then came dialysis, initiated in America by Dr. Wilhelm Kolff at the Cleveland Clinic. The cost of this was soon taken over by Medicare and Medicaid. Sixty thousand people are now on dialysis at an annual cost of $1.8 billion, 3.6 percent of all Medicare costs, and the numbers and costs are still rising.

And what of the artificial heart? The cost of supporting Barney Clark for four months of existence was $200,000.

Transplantations

What will happen when transplantation operations, some of them costing $100,000 or more, become routine for anyone with failing heart, liver, lungs or kidneys? The liver and lungs are two of the most common sites of metastasis from cancers. Will everyone who has cancer of the liver or lung be eligible for a transplantation? If not, who will decide who will be given the chance to live? The ethics and economies of medicine pose terrible questions that will have to be confronted.

One thing is certain: We cannot anticipate an average life span of more than 100 years even if all diseases become curable. This is because the life of a brain cell is finite, and the cell can never reproduce itself. Eternal or even a great prolongation of life is a dream that is based on fantasy, not fact. But it looks as if it would be easy enough to spend half of our gross national product on what might be largely futile medical diagnosis and treatment.

As an alternative, would it be better to spend a tenth of this sum on research into the cause of disease? Could we eliminate many of the most fatal of all cancers by making it impossible for anyone to smoke cigarettes? Could we reduce the incidence of

123

Devices for the Wealthy

Can America afford to develop a workable artificial heart? It has been estimated that the device, the operation and the hospital care would cost $100,000 per recipient in the first year after implantation. With projections of the number of recipients ranging from 16,000 to 66,000 each year, the total annual cost would run between $1.6 billion and $6.6 billion. At a time when the Federal budget is strained, when the deficit is approaching $200 billion and when many Federal health programs are being cut back, the nation cannot afford these additional expenditures.

Yet if the artificial heart is perfected and the government is unwilling to pay for the operations of all who need it, the device will be available only to the wealthy, who already receive better health care than the poor do.

Dr. Barton J. Bernstein, professor of history, Stanford University, in *The Nation* magazine, 1983

the next most fatal cancers, those of the colon and rectum, by seeing to it that there was adequate fiber in the diet? Could we reduce the incidence of breast cancer by reducing the fat in the diet?

We are indeed at a crossroads. There is no way that we can continue indefinitely to spend more and more money on developing machines that diagnose diseases that we cannot cure or in designing artificial organs or in perfecting the technique of transplanting organs that, if they were widely employed, would result in an almost incalculable expense.

Hope for lengthening life expectancy lies more in basic research than in clinical trials. We need to find a chemical that can be carried by monoclonal antibodies to the specific cancer cell against which it is directed. And we need to find a chemical whose presence or absence is the cause of arterial disease. Money spent on such projects might be more productive than fostering the proliferation of scanners and artificial organs.

ORGAN DONATION IS THE KEY

Robert M. Veatch

Robert Veatch is a professor of Medical Ethics at Georgetown University's Kennedy Institute of Ethics, a research center devoted to studying the social and ethical aspects of medicine and health policy. He has graduate level training in neuropharmacology, a divinity school degree from Harvard, and a doctorate in the study of religion and society at Harvard where he concentrated in medical ethics. In the following statement he reviews the bioethical and religious issues surrounding organ procurement.

Points to Consider

1. Under what circumstances is organ procurement from living donors acceptable?
2. How do religious groups feel about removal of organs for life saving purposes from human bodies that have been established as dead?
3. What is the controversy of donation vs. the salvaging of organs about?
4. What method for organ procurement does the author favor?

Robert M. Veatch in testimony before the Subcommittee on Investigations and Oversight, 1983.

125

Any scheme that abandons the mode of donation in favor of viewing the cadaver as a social resource to be mined for worthwhile social purposes will directly violate central tenets of Christian thought and create serious problems for Jews.

Although I am a Methodist, I speak for no religious or academic group and shall try to present fairly my understanding of the views of major religious groups on the issues at hand.

The bioethical debate over organ procurement goes back at least to the first kidney transplants in 1954. The current generation of controversy, however, can be dated from December 3, 1967, when Christiaan Barnard transplanted the first human heart into the chest of Louis Washkansky. In what follows I limit my remarks to the procurement of **cadaver** organs. While organ procurement from living donors, especially related donors, appears to be acceptable in cases where the transplant would be life-saving for a recipient and would not be life-threatening for the donor, there is widespread disapproval of procuring organs from living donors when the removal of the organ would be life-threatening.

In any case, I assume that cadaver organ procurement constitutes the critical ethical and public policy problem. It is here that the most good can be done by clarifying our ethical and religious requirements . . .

Religious Groups

All major religious groups reveal some differences of opinion over a shift to the use of a brain-oriented definition of death, a shift important if organ procurement is to be facilitated. Within Judaism there has been the greatest resistance to shifting to a brain-oriented definition of death. Rabbi David Bleich, philosopher at Yeshiva University, for example, opposes any shift, saying that "the patient cannot be pronounced dead other than upon the irreversible cessation of both cardiac and respiratory activity." On the other hand, other Rabbis from Conservative and Reformed traditions have endorsed the use of brain criteria for death pronouncement.

Among Catholics Pope Pius XII opened the door for a shift in the definition of death in 1957 saying, "it remains for the doctor, and especially the anesthesiologist, to give a clear and precise definition of 'death' and the 'moment of death' of a patient who passes away in a state of unconsciousness." There have never

126

been any principled theological objections to a brain-oriented definition of death among Catholics although occasionally more conservative Catholics, often those associated with right-to-life positions, have expressed fear that acknowledging that a person is dead when the brain is dead might indirectly lessen respect for those who are still living.

Protestant theologians (and Protestant groups when they have spoken on the subject) have almost uniformly favored some brain-oriented definition of death whether they represent more conservative (Paul Ramsey) or liberal (Joseph Fletcher) perspectives. Thus while there is some concern about the use of a brain-oriented definition of death, at least some responsible members of all major religious traditions accept it theologically and find it appropriate as a basis for procuring cadaver organs.

More significantly, there is substantial ethical agreement on the second preliminary ethical question, the ethics of removal of cadaver organs. There has in general been no objection among either the secular or religious bioethical community to the removal of organs for life-saving purposes from human bodies once it is established those persons are dead.

The Core Issues

This brings us to the more critical and controversial core ethical issues. First, the controversy over donation vs. salvaging of organs. It has been recognized for years that there are two basic

127

alternatives for organ procurement: donation and salvaging. Under salvaging schemes, such as that proposed by Dukeminier and Sanders, cadaver organs would be routinely made available as needed as a social resource. Normally, advocates of salvaging would permit individuals to object in writing while living or even permit relatives to object in cases where the individual has not expressed his or her wishes. The other alternative emphasizes donation.

It is this second alternative that has been favored by virtually every writer within the Judeo-Christian tradition and by every religious group speaking on the subject. The reason is fundamentally that according to the Judeo-Christian tradition, our respect for the individual and the rights associated with that individual do not cease at death. Obligations of respect—for the wishes of the deceased and the integrity of his earthly remains—must continue. In the Judeo-Christian tradition, as opposed to much pagan Greek thought, the body is affirmed to be a central part of the total spiritual being. Any scheme that abandons the mode of donation in favor of viewing the cadaver as a social resource to be mined for worthwhile social purposes will directly violate central tenets of Christian thought and create serious problems for Jews as well, especially in a state not based on Jewish law. It will predictably produce vociferous, agitated opposition. While I cannot predict street riots comparable to those sparked in Israel after the passing of autopsy laws permitting routine violations of the corpse, it is safe to say there would be sustained and vocal opposition.

Uniform Support

At the same time there is uniform support in all major traditions not only for the ethical acceptability of donation, but the actual moral obligation to take organ donation seriously. This suggests while, for practical and theoretical reasons, all traditions would oppose routine salvaging, they would look favorably upon public policies to make donation as easy as possible. Given the fact that these religious traditions all support organ donation in at least some circumstances and in fact consider it a morally weighty obligation, they would favor public policies making it as easy as possible to express a willingness to donate organs for life-saving purposes.

The public policy implication is that the correct solution to the donation vs. salvaging controversy is maximum encouragement to facilitate donation, provided this does not subtly coerce those unwilling to donate or does not trick them into donating unintentionally. The schemes to indicate willingness to donate on state drivers' licenses, for example, would seem very reason-

> **The public policy implication is that the correct solution to the donation versus salvaging controversy is maximum encouragement to facilitate donation, provided that this does not subtly coerce those unwilling to donate or trick them into donating without realizing it.**
>
> **The schemes to indicate willingness to donate on State driver's licenses, for example, seem very reasonable.**

able. In addition, questions on federal documents, especially those already computerized for easy retrieval such as income tax or social security records, would seem appropriate. The ideal form of the question about willingness to donate would permit three responses—yes, no, and no response—thus not creating any presumptions or pressures on any respondents. This strategy seems far preferable to continental European public policies authorizing routine salvaging unless objection has been registered. It is even preferable to the scheme endorsed by the British Working Party of the Health Departments of Great Britain and Northern Ireland, which would give a designated government or hospital official the power to remove organs for transplantation in cases where no objection has been registered and relatives cannot be located. This group who die alone, without relatives available, is sufficiently small and sufficiently vulnerable that those formulating public policies should bend over backwards to avoid abusing their right to be treated with maximum respect.

23

PRESUMED CONSENT IS NECESSARY

Peter Safar

Peter Safar is a physician, "Distinguished Service Professor of Resuscitation Medicine," and director of the Resuscitation Research Center of the University of Pittsburgh. He is engaged almost fulltime in research on acute dying processes and their reversibility. His research programs are in the laboratory, with patients, and in the community. He was the initiator and chairman of the Department of Anesthesiology and Critical Care Medicine at the University of Pittsburgh and before that, Chief Anesthesiologist at the Baltimore City Hospitals, where he and his associates developed America's first physician-staffed medical-surgical intensive care unit.

Points to Consider

1. How serious will the problem of a shortage of organ donors become?
2. What is the present procedure for organ procurement like?
3. Who was Emperor Joseph II and what law did he establish?
4. What is "presumed consent" and why does the author favor this procedure for organ procurement?

Excerpted from testimony by Peter Safar before the House Subcommittee on Investigations and Oversight, 1983.

130

Presumed consent would probably be an effective mechanism to overcome inertia and increase organ procurement.

Since I am not a transplant surgeon, I have no vested interests. My testimony will reflect my personal knowledge, attitudes and values, based on experiences with patient care, teaching, research, administration and program initiation . . .

Recipients

For end stage renal failure, about 62,000 patients are presently on dialysis; about 5,000 patients received kidney transplants last year in the USA.

Since the introduction of cyclosporine for suppression of the immune rejection of transplanted organs in 1980, about 100 kidneys per year are transplanted at the Presbyterian-University Hospital in Pittsburgh, with an over 80% graft survival rate; 94% of the patients survived.

Once the immune rejection problem is solved, the need for multi-organ donors may increase to 50–100,000 per year in the USA. While about 50% of the 62,000 patients with end stage renal failure now on dialysis, i.e., 30,000, are estimated to be suitable recipients, the number of candidates for heart transplants may become even greater. Transplantations of hearts can be expected to mushroom once the operative mortality and rejection rate drops below about 20%. Most likely, artificial heart devices will prove to be effective more for temporary artificial circulation while the patient with a failing heart is evaluated as to the recuperability of his own heart, or is being considered for transplantation. Transplanted hearts seem to adapt better than presently available artificial hearts to changes in functional demands.

Because of the sensitivity of vital organs to a reduction in the supply of oxygen and nutrients, the transplantation of viable kidneys, hearts, lungs, livers, pancreases, etc., requires procurement of organs from brain dead cadavers with the heart kept beating by breathing machine. To meet the above mentioned need for 50–100,000 multi-organ donors per year in the near future, methods will have to be found to increase the procurement of organs suitable for transplantation. In recent years, organs were procured from only about 2500 brain dead donors per year in the USA. The estimated maximal number of brain dead donors presently available is about 20,000 per year in the U.S.A. This estimate is based on about 2% of the 1 million deaths which occur each year in our nation's hospitals (another 1 million deaths per year occur outside hospitals). At present only an

131

estimated 5,000 patients received organ transplantations last year in the U.S.A. In 1981, 3,400 kidneys were transplanted, while 6,000 patients are on waiting lists. This figure should be higher considering the estimated 30,000 suitable candidates for kidney transplantation. Methods have to be devised to increase the number of donors and to make maximal use of available donor organs . . .

Present Organ Procurement

In most major medical centers with advanced intensive care units patients who develop brain death (e.g., from trauma, oxygen lack, stroke, tumor) are managed as recommended. This includes a detailed orderly determination of brain death according to clearly spelled out criteria, certification of brain death by two physicians not of the transplant team, obtaining of consent from the next of kin to remove organs for transplantation, and finally operative removal of organs from the heart beating cadaver prior to discontinuing the ventilator. This safe and orderly process is not always followed in some community hospitals, as illustrated by an occasional patient in the past transferred to our hospital for organ transplantation, with the diagnosis of brain death, in whom the prescribed orderly examination revealed that he was not brain dead, and continued life support resulted in recovery. There also seem to be physicians who because of not wanting to be bothered or because of fear of malpractice suits, shy away from initiating brain death certification and rather let nature take its course.

Voluntary donation by family members has, in the experience of Grenvik's group at Pittsburgh, posed no major problems. The majority of families approached at the time of brain death certification have considered organ donation a positive act, to give the life and death of the deceased additional meaning. These positive feelings were seen in spite of shock and grief. Nevertheless, about 1 of 5 families of potential donors' approached by others have refused donations. Hesitancy on the part of primary physicians to approach the family during shock and grief, when he the physician has a feeling of failure in the face of the patient's demise, understandably adds to a low organ procurement rate.

The carrying of donor cards has not been effective since "our own death is indeed unimaginable" (Freud) and people prefer not to plan for it. Education of physicians, particularly those controlling brain death certification in intensive care units, has been effective but should be intensified to include those responsible for the care of ICU patients in community hospitals. Financial incentives given by Medicare reimbursement schemes and re-

132

Coercive Steps Needed

What has to happen from now on is a gentle boost in public consciousness together with properly timed coercive steps. I have in mind a goal demanding individuals to state yes or no to organ donation at the time they renew their Driver's License without the need for witnesses and with full legal recognition that a transplant surgeon may proceed to remove organs from an individual carrying a "yes" card without the fear of prosecution.

Dr. G. Melville Williams, professor of surgery, Johns Hopkins Hospital in Baltimore, congressional testimony, 1983

quirements of hospital accreditation boards for orderly brain death determination would help in the procurement of a greater number of organs from brain dead potential donors in not only transplant hospitals, but the majority of hospitals nationwide. There should be increasing consideration given to the transfer of heart beating cadavers to transplantation hospitals for multiple organ procurement. This donor transfer is needed for heart and lung transplants, since the lungs must be transplanted within one hour. Transfer would have to be carried out by mobile ICU ambulances staffed with paramedics under physician direction.

Presumed Consent

Historically, Emperor Joseph II of Austria in the 1700s established a law (which still prevails in Europe) which enables doctors to perform autopsies on patients who die in hospitals, to determine the cause of death and enhance scientific knowledge, without asking for consent. The patient's relatives, however, could refuse, which very rarely happened. This presumed consent for autopsy was used widely by European medical researchers since the mid-1800s for pioneering great advances in medicine. In my own efforts to improve emergency medical services in the U.S.A., I have frequently been frustrated by the inability to determine the cause of death and the potential salvagability of a victim of acute illness or injury. Autopsies are needed for quality control of care and for gaining new knowledge to advance the therapeutic potentials of medicine. In the U.S.A., only in cases of suspected mishaps or a wrong doing will the medical

133

examiner or coroner get involved; only he may use implied consent for autopsy. In some states this includes implied permission to remove eyes or other organs from the cadaver. For transplantation, the general health of donors should be established by autopsy. The operation of organ removal in a way represents a partial autopsy while the heart is beating. Transplantation would benefit from at least giving medical examiners automatic permission to remove organs, and to delegate autopsies and organ removal to the hospital.

Presumed consent would probably be an effective mechanism to overcome inertia and increase organ procurement. It is possible that in the U.S.A. such presumed consent legislation would be declared unconstitutional. The presumed consent for autopsy has in recent years in some European countries been expanded to a presumed consent for organ donation. A recent review (Stuart, et al.) revealed that these countries include Austria, Czechoslovakia, Denmark, France, Israel, Poland and Switzerland. There is a trend that other European countries will follow, as presumed consent has been recommended by the European Committee on Legal Cooperation (equivalent to our National Conference on Uniform State Laws). In my opinion, automatic permission for hospital physicians to carry out autopsies and organ donation (unless the family objects) without having to solicit consent from the family, would facilitate measures which are in the public interest, would advance knowledge for improving life-saving measures, would permit use of donor organs to keep others alive, and would merely represent a generalization of the already existing regulations under which medical examiners and coroners function in this country. Because of the deeply rooted voluntarism in the U.S.A., however, before embarking on a promotion of presumed consent legislation, it may be wise to carry out an opinion poll to prevent a backlash, which would result in increased public refusal of organ donation.

SELLING HUMAN ORGANS

H. Barry Jacobs vs. Ellen Goodman

*H. Barry Jacobs, M.D., is the medical director of the International Kidney Exchange, Ltd. Ellen Goodman is a political commentator and columnist for **The Boston Globe**. In the following point and counterpoint exchange, the merits of buying and selling body parts are debated. H. Barry Jacobs claims the profit motive can solve the kidney shortage. Ellen Goodman believes that buying and selling organs would be a ghoulish business.*

Points to Consider

1. How might the profit motive help solve the shortage of kidneys for transplant operations?
2. What does H. Barry Jacobs say about the moral issue of selling kidneys?
3. How does Ellen Goodman say our system of values relates to the selling of body parts?
4. What specific reasons does she give for opposition to the sale of organs?

THE POINT—by H. Barry Jacobs

The International Kidney Exchange was formed to meet the needs of 70,000 Americans suffering and dying while handcuffed to dehumanizing kidney dialysis machines.

Because of shortages of kidneys, transplant operations help fewer than one out of 10 patients. For years, the existing "voluntary donor" system has been a dismal failure.

The majority of the 5,000 kidneys that are transplanted each year come from 2,200 brain-dead citizens. It is not our intent to interfere with this limited source of kidneys.

God gave us two kidneys. We need only one-half of one kidney to live a normal, healthy life. And God gave us the intelligence and ability to perform kidney transplantation operations.

Profit Motive

The profit motive, which is nothing new to organized medicine, is an additional way to solve the shortage. In fact, our government has agreed to fund a pilot program to compensate 300 healthy living kidney donors, who are not related to the organ recipients, and also to pay the donors' service fees.

Each year, kidney dialysis costs taxpayers more than $2 billion. Eighty-five percent of transplanted kidneys will function for more than five years. Each additional kidney transplant will save $142,000 in dialysis costs over five years and end misery, suffering and substantial risk.

We service American recipients by bringing together only consenting adults. Their physicians choose the best match and perform the surgery. We do not participate in their fee arrangement or medical decisions. We have a standard fee, $5,000, for our services.

Assuming the government pays the service fee for indigent patients, there could be no incentive to help the rich. If made illegal, only the rich could go overseas to obtain a transplant.

The Moral Issue

Some doctors raise the moral issue of risk when money is involved, but imply the risk is less for volunteers. The risk for serious injury or death is less than 1 per 1,000 donors. It is the responsibility of the operating surgeons to fully inform both donors and recipients of their respective risks.

Stress from any cause, including financial trouble, increases the risks for disease.

Compensating the donor for blood or a kidney is the American way. Many jobs, such as that of a coal miner, have certain risks for lung disease and injury. Yet, they made informed decisions to do those jobs.

When it comes to deciding what to do with our bodies, Congress is not a better judge than the individual. In the end, the kidney debate should be resolved by individual doctors and their patients, not by politicians. Only in the Soviet Union do human organs belong to the State.

THE COUNTERPOINT—by Ellen Goodman

When my daughter was small, I used to sing an old, bittersweet lullaby about life and death. There was a line of fatalism that ran through this song: "If livin' were a thing that money could buy, the rich would live and the poor would die."

A Hippocratic oath

By David Seavey, USA TODAY

I remember that line because living often is a thing that money can buy. We see this not just in photographs from the Third World but sometimes in stories from our own world. Lately, we have witnessed it when communities from Massachusetts to Wyoming tried to raise funds the way they once raised barns, for a neighbor who needed a life-saving heart or liver transplant.

Rich and Poor

But never has the relationship between rich and poor, life and death, been so crassly presented as in the latest venture of a Virginia doctor who set up a business to broker human kidneys. Under this scheme a person who needed the money could literally sell a kidney to a person who needed the organ, and the doctor would get a fee for his services.

I suppose it was inevitable in this world of supply and demand that someone would seize such a ghoulish business opportunity. Not long ago, in Maine, a man set up a short-lived plan under which people could have their organs sold after death and the benefits sent to a beneficiary. Last summer, a Wall Street Journal columnist suggested that private and government health insurance agencies pay relatives some money for the organs of the deceased.

More than 6,000 people are waiting for kidney transplants; more than 4,000 await corneas. The next logical step of the free-enterprise system would surely allow a live person with two kidneys, two corneas and a mess of debts to sell what he or she owns. Whose body is it, after all?

But there are limits to what is tolerable. To some degree our society has permitted the buying and selling of bodies. We have supported prostitution, allowed the purchase of sperm and blood, and witnessed contracts for ova and rental of wombs. But we have not yet permitted human beings to be stripped of organs for profit. We have never accepted the notion that the have-nots should become a source of spare parts for the haves.

As Daniel Callahan, the director of the Hastings Center which deals with questions of medical ethics says, "In theory there ought to be no laws that would stop competent adults from selling whatever they want. But the potential for abuse is just too great."

The fundamental abuse is, of course, exploitation of people so desperate that they would sell half their sight or kidney function. But there are other troubling questions: If a person can sell a kidney, should he or she be able to sell a heart? If an organ is up for sale, should it go for the top dollar?

138

Our Values

"Our system of values isn't supposed to allow the auctioning off of life to the highest bidder," says Rep. Albert Gore Jr., D-Tenn. "It erodes the distinction between things and people. It's not too difficult to conjure up some great problems in the future if we place a bounty on human organs."

For these reasons Gore has added a prohibition against buying or selling organs from live or dead people to a new bill governing organ procurement. But he knows that these bizarre market schemes are emerging only because of the intense need and competition for transplants.

In the current scramble for organs, the gap between the rich and poor isn't the only one. There is the gap between those who have access to publicity—like the parents of Jamie Fiske, who recently underwent a liver transplant at University of Minnesota Hospitals—and those who have not.

And there is the fundamental gap between the large source of potential donors and the small number of actual donations. Each year there are about 20,000 potential donors—people who have suffered brain death—and only about 2,500 who ultimately provide organs for transplants. The latest Gallup Polls show that 95 percent of Americans know about the shortage of organs, but only 24 percent would give permission for organs to be donated.

The notion of merchandising organs is an unseemly and inhuman one. But in the end, the problem isn't whether we can buy life, but how we can be persuaded to give it.

POTENTIAL
ORGAN DONOR SURVEY

This activity may be used as an individualized study guide for students in libraries and resource centers or as a discussion catalyst in small groups and classroom discussions.

Guidelines

The Uniform Anatomical Gifts Act permits a person to donate his or her kidneys, heart, liver, eyes, and other organs upon death to others who need organ transplant operations.

a. Complete the potential organ donor survey below.

b. Working in small groups, find the questions that members do not agree on. Discuss why the disagreements exist.

c. Compile the results of the survey for the whole class.

d. Make a project out of giving the survey to 100 people, classifying them and the results by age, sex and educational background.

The Survey

1. Do you currently carry an organ donor card?
   _____ yes   _____ no

2. Would you, if asked, be prepared to sign and carry an organ donor card?
   _____ yes   _____ no

3. If you had to make the decision, would you donate the organs of a relative who had just died?
   _____ yes   _____ no

4. If you were to die suddenly, do you think that your family would give permission for the removal of any of your organs for transplantation?
   _____ yes   _____ no

Excerpted from the National Heart Transplantation Study, Potential Organ Donor Survey, Hearings before the House Subcommittee on Investigations and Oversight, 1983.

5. Which, if any, of the following organs would you be willing to donate? Would you be willing to donate . . .

_____ kidneys   _____ lungs
_____ corneas   _____ pancreas
_____ heart   _____ skin
_____ liver   _____ whole body

6. Do you feel that if someone signs an organ donor card his or her decision should have to be formally approved by his next-of-kin when he dies?

_____ yes   _____ no

7. If the next of kin disapproves do you feel that their disapproval should override the potential donor's wishes as expressed on any organ donor card?

_____ yes   _____ no

8. Do you feel that the next-of-kin should be allowed to donate the organs of relatives who have recently died but have **not** signed an organ donor card?

_____ yes   _____ no

9. Do you feel that doctors should have the power to remove organs from people who have recently died but have **not** signed an organ donor card without consulting their next-of-kin?

_____ yes   _____ no

10. Brain death is considered to occur when brain activity stops, although it is possible to continue heartbeat and respiration by artificial means. State laws may use brain death as the legal definition of death and will allow the removal of organs for transplantation, such as the heart, from persons pronounced dead on such a basis. Do you feel that brain death should be used as the legal definition of death?

_____ yes   _____ no

11. Do you feel that it is all right to remove organs for transplantation upon declaration of brain death?

_____ yes   _____ no

12. Do you feel that individuals should be allowed to sell organs in the same way that people sell blood, or sperm for insemination?

_____ yes   _____ no

13. Would you consider selling organs from the bodies of deceased family members, or nonvital organs of your own?

_____ yes   _____ no

BIBLIOGRAPHY

Annas, George J. "Help from the Dead: The Cases of Brother Fox and John Storar." **Hastings Center Report** vol. 11 (June, 1981) pp. 19–20.

Annas, George J. "Nonfeeding: Lawful Killing in California, Homicide in New Jersey." **Hastings Center Report** vol. 13 (December, 1983) pp. 19–20.

Assisted Suicide: The Compassionate Crime. (Los Angeles, CA: Hemlock Society).

Baer, Louis Shattuck, M.D. **Let the Patient Decide. A Doctor's Advice to Older Persons.** (Westminster Philadelphia Press, 1978).

Barber, Bernard. **Informed Consent in Medical Therapy and Research.** (New Brunswick, NJ: Rutgers University Press, 1980).

Beauchamp, Tom L., and Seymour Perlin, eds. **Ethical Issues in Death and Dying.** (Englewood Cliffs, NJ: Prentice-Hall, 1978).

Bok, S. "Personal Directions for Care at the End of Life." **New England Journal of Medicine** 295 (1976) pp. 367–69.

Callahan, Daniel. "On Feeding the Dying." **Hastings Center Report** vol. 13 (October, 1983) p. 22.

Caplan, Arthur. "Organ Transplants: The Costs of Success." **Hastings Center Report** vol. 13 (December, 1983) pp. 23–32.

Childress, James F. **Priorities in Biomedical Ethics.** (Philadelphia, PA; Westminster Press, 1981).

Coffin, Margaret M. **Death in Early America: The History and Folklore of Customs and Superstitions of Early Medicine, Funerals, Burials and Mourning.** (Nashville, NY, 1976).

Davidson, G. E., ed. **Living With Dying.** (Minneapolis: Augsburg, 1978).

Delahoyde, Melinda and Dennis Horan, eds. **Infanticide and the Handicapped Newborn.** (Provo, UT: Brigham Young Univ., 1982).

Denny, Donald. "How Organs Are Distributed." **Hastings Center Report** vol. 13 (December, 1983) pp. 26–27.

Devine, Philip E. **The Ethics of Homicide.** (Ithaca, NY: Cornell University Press, 1978).

Fried, C. "Terminating Life Support: Out of the Closet." **New England Journal of Medicine** vol. 295 (1976) pp. 390–91.

Garton, Jean Staker. **Who Broke the Baby?** (Minnesota: Bethany House, 1979).

Graves, Frances A. "Can Suicide Be Rational?" **Hastings Center Report** vol. 12 (June, 1982) p. 45.

"Guidelines for the Determination of Death: Report of the Medical Consultants on the Diagnosis of Death to the President's Commission for the Study of Ethical Problems in Medicine and Biomedical and Behavioral Research." **Journal of the American Medical Association** 246 (1981) pp. 2184–86.

Harron, Burnside, and Beauchamp. **Health and Human Values.** (New Haven, CT: Yale Univ. Press, 1983).

Hilfiker, D. "Allowing the Debilitated to Die: Facing Our Ethical Choices. **New England Journal of Medicine** 308 (1983) pp. 716–19.

Humphrey, Derek. **Let Me Die Before I Wake.** (Los Angeles, CA: Hemlock Society, 1982).

Jackson, D. L. and S. Youngner. "Patient Autonomy and 'Death with Dignity': Some Clinical Caveats." **New England Journal of Medicine** 301 (1979) pp. 404–408.

Kamisar, Yale. "Some Non-religious Views Against Proposed 'Mercy-Killing' Legislation." **Minnesota Law Review** 42 (1958) pp. 969, 1010–11.

Koop, C. Everett and Francis A. Schaeffer. **Whatever Happened to the Human Race?** (Westchester, IL: Crossway Books, 1983).

Kubler-Ross, Elisabeth. **Death the Final Stage of Growth.** (New Jersey: Prentice Hall, 1975).

Kubler-Ross, Elisabeth. **On Death and Dying.** (New York: Macmillan, 1969).

"Living Wills: Need for Legal Recognition." **West Virginia Law Review** 78 (1977) pp. 370, 380.

Lynn, Joanne and James F. Childress. "Must Patients Always Be Given Food and Water?" **Hastings Center Report** vol. 13 (October, 1983) pp. 17–21.

Martinson, Ida M. and William F. Henry. "Home Care for Dying Children." **Hastings Center Report** vol. 10 (April, 1980) pp. 5–7.

Miller, Bruce L. "Autonomy and the Refusal of Lifesaving Treatment." **Hastings Center Report** vol. 11 (August, 1981) pp. 22–28.

Mitford, Jessica. **The American Way of Death.** (New York: Pantheon Books, 1973).

"Optimum Care for Hopelessly Ill Patients: A Report of the Clinical Care Committee of the Massachusetts General Hospital." **New England Journal of Medicine** 295 (1976) pp. 362–64.

President's Commission for the Study of Ethical Problems in Medicine and Biomedical and Behavioral Research. **Deciding to Forego Life-Sustaining Treatment.** (Washington, DC: Government Printing Office, 1983) pp. 236–39.

Quinlan, Joseph and Julia. **Karen Ann.** (Garden City, NY: Doubleday, 1977).

Rachels, James. "Barney Clark's Key." **Hastings Center Report** vol. 13 (April, 1983) pp. 17–19.

Relman, A.S. "Michigan's Sensible 'Living Will'." **New England Journal of Medicine** 300 (1979) pp. 1270–72.

Silverman, William A. "Mismatched Attitudes about Neonatal Death." **Hastings Center Report** vol. 11 (December, 1981) pp. 12–16.

Smith, David H. and Judith A. Granbois. "The American Way of Hospice." **Hastings Center Report** vol. 12 (April, 1982) pp. 8–10.

Society for the Right to Die. **Handbook of Enacted Laws.** (New York, NY).

Steinfels, Peter and Robert M. Veatch, eds. **Death Inside Out.** (New York: Harper and Row, 1974).

Stoddard, Sandol. **The Hospice Movement. A Better Way of Caring for the Dying.** (New York: Stein and Day, 1978).

"Swiss OK Mercy Death: Reject Abortion." **National Right to Life News** (December, 1977) p. 9.

Veatch, Robert M. **Death, Dying and the Biological Revolution.** (New Haven, CT: Yale University Press, 1976).

Wiesman, Avery D. **On Dying and Denying: A Psychiatric Study of Terminality.** (New York: Behavioral Publications, Inc., 1972).

Worden, J. William and William Proctor. **Personal Death Awareness.** (New Jersey: Prentice-Hall, 1976).